My Glass is Always Half Full

When I travel life's journey

With faith and gratitude

Marianne Laska (signature)

Marianne Laska

Acknowledgements

How does one begin to thank the many people that came along on my journey, some from the beginning, others at the halfway point and yet others cheering me on at the finish line?

First and foremost, I thank my God for carrying me through the many twists and turns of this journey and faithfully providing me with the strength I needed.

Secondly, I thank my wonderful husband, Bob, for being my constant companion, accurate note taker at doctor visits, and whose constant love and encouragement made it possible for me to keep going and not get stuck on my journey.

And next, not only my two wonderful, caring sons, Brian and Keith, for always being there when I needed them, but also their beautiful life partners, Kathy and Carrie, for being the compassionate daughters I never had, but who entered my life at the perfect time.

Last, but certainly not least, and there are not enough positive adjectives to describe them: my beautiful seven-year old granddaughter, Chloe, and handsome four-year old grandson, Bradley. Even though they were not a part of the journey, they truly were the prize at the finish line!

In order not to leave anyone out I have decided that, except for my immediate family, not to mention by name the many doctors, nurses and many other companions on my journey. I am sure they will recognize themselves and realize how grateful I am for the incredible part they played in my healing process.

Foreword

During difficult times, friends and acquaintances, wanting to be supportive, share their favorite expressions of encouragement: from phrases such as, "When life hands you lemons, make lemonade," to the more eloquent, "Character cannot be developed in ease and quiet. Only through experience of trial and suffering can the soul be strengthened, ambition inspired, and success achieved."(Hellen Keller).

As the eternal optimist, I have embraced the phrase, "The glass is always half full," since I truly believe that when unexpected difficulties enter your life you have one of two choices: Either seeing it as a stumbling block and making you bitter, or seeing it as a stepping stone and making you better. I have chosen the latter.

My book, *"My Glass is Always Half Full,"* is about serious illnesses, difficult times and many other happenings that could have easily made me bitter, but instead the opposite is true. I decided to chronicle my journey with factual details, intermittent happenings, intertwined with the all-important humor in any situation, and above all, gratitude.

Research has shown that only a small fraction of people's happiness is due to circumstances and only by practicing gratitude can the gap be filled. As a daughter of parents who survived the horrors of WW II in Europe, I was taught this attribute at an early age, and always by their example. It never ceases to amaze me that the

4

simplicity of this gift of gratitude has been so life giving to me, allowing me to be at peace in the middle of the storms of my life.

The writing of this book was encouraged by a friend who admired my positive attitude and encouraged me to document my journey. I was not so sure as I thought that my "the glass is always half full" attitude might annoy some people, but she assured me by saying that maybe I would be able to fill their half empty glass.

I invite you to come on the journey with me! You might find out that your glass is half full already, and if not, maybe I will be able in some small way make it fuller than before.

Table of Contents

Introduction

It is hard to believe it has been more than 16 years since my last breast cancer diagnosis, and I always meant to chronicle the events in writing.

My first thought was that I would do so at my five year mark of survival, but that came and went, then the 10 year anniversary seemed like a good idea to start this project, but that never came to fruition either. It was not until of late that I received encouragement from several people who were touched by my positive attitude and felt that I should document my story as it would be an inspiration to others walking this journey. As mentioned in the foreword, one special friend was the deciding factor by making me aware that my positive attitude might yet be another way for me to encourage someone who was stuck on their journey. I must admit I never thought about it that way.

I am not someone who is into journaling, but had saved all the calendars of those years. Going through these to look for dates, appointments and other happenings in order to create an outline for this book, I was amazed how all the details were still so vivid in my mind and I just started writing.

When I was initially diagnosed with breast cancer, I had been a nurse for more than 30 years. I remember admitting women around my age to the department I worked in and who were diagnosed with cancer. I would look over the face sheet of their paperwork with their name and all the other pertinent information, but what always seemed to glare at me was the diagnosis of cancer placed in the lower right hand corner. I remember thinking, "if not for the grace of God, this could be me", and then, in December 1997, it was.

1

Start of the Journey

December 1997

I was sitting at the kitchen table reminiscing about how wonderful the last few weeks had been. We celebrated Thanksgiving in Massachusetts with my older son Brian, his fiancée Kathy, her parents, Dave and Janet, and grandparents Colin and Bina. We have a very small family and we always appreciate getting together and enjoying each other's company.

Immediately following Thanksgiving, my husband, Bob, and I flew to France to visit our younger son, Keith, who had made the decision to study abroad during his junior year at the College of the Holy Cross. He also decided to live with a family instead of in a dorm in order to fully immerse himself in the culture, and we were amazed how much he had adjusted to everything in just a few short months. During the day, while Keith was at the university, Bob and I did some sightseeing and Bob's and my limited high school French did help to order meals and ask for directions. We also found that the French people really appreciated us trying to speak their language and, thankfully, quickly helped us out with responses in English. Evenings were no problem since Keith, by now fluent in French, became our tour guide and we enjoyed exploring the area that had become his temporary home.

However, it was back to reality. One of my nurse friends called me and asked if I would like to join her and some other nurses for lunch. I thanked her, but declined as I was scheduled for my yearly mammogram that day and since I still was a little jet-lagged and had to work the 11-7 P.M. shift that night, my time would be better served with a good long nap. I took a shower, remembering not to apply deodorant, and went on my way to what I thought would be just another yearly mammogram.

It was not to be. Several hours later I received a call from my medical doctor with the news that there were calcifications on this mammogram, which was a definite change from the one of the previous year. "You need to call a surgeon, Marianne" she added. I have known this doctor for many years, as a nurse and a patient, and was hoping to get some reassuring additional words that would calm my pounding heart. I asked, "How soon do you want me to see the surgeon" and she responded,

"As soon as possible". I had my answer, and it was not what I wanted to hear.

I called the surgeon I would be most comfortable with. I had observed her compassion with patients in the hospital we both worked in, and, ironically, she and I had been working on a care plan regarding post-operative guidelines for women diagnosed with breast cancer. I do not think I made much sense when I called the office for an appointment. All I kept thinking "I might have cancer" and questions about my insurance and other details needed to make this appointment seemed, in my humble opinion, totally unnecessary at this time. Of course I knew better, took a deep breath, pulled myself together and provided the information in order to pave the way for an appointment.

In my state of mind, sleep was totally out of the question as well as going to work that night and be responsible for very ill patients. I still cannot believe how easy that decision was. Calling in to work was not something I took very lightly and had seldom done in the past 28 years at the hospital I was employed in.

I was able to get an appointment the next day and Bob and I went together. My surgeon was very reassuring as we went through my history and the likelihood of my calcifications actually being breast cancer. Late start of period, check, children prior to age 30, check, nursed both children, check again! After several other questions with also positive check marks, I started to feel a little more positive. With my health history I had an 80% chance to be in the "no breast cancer calcification" percentile, which I thought were pretty good odds. She said the office would call with a date for my lumpectomy, which would probably be just before Christmas.

Now there was something positive! The timing of my surgery would give me Christmas and New Year off, an unheard phenomenon in the nursing profession. "You are going to be just fine," Bob said, as we were leaving the office. I nodded and smiled, but the nagging feeling somehow persisted. On the way home, I turned to Bob and said, "I really wish I could talk to my mother". Bob looked worried, as he should, since my mother had passed away more than ten years before, and said, "You know that is not possible, right"? I knew that but the words came out of my mouth before giving it another thought. My mother had this amazing ability to shed a positive light on any circumstance and I just needed to hear her say that all would be well.

We arrived home and I called my older son, Brian, and some close friends to update them on the situation. I decided, because of the time difference, to call my son, Keith, the next morning. There was an initial silence on the other end of the line as all were trying to digest this unexpected news. Having gotten my bearings at this point, I was able to convince them and myself that all would be well. After all, I am my mother's daughter and a positive attitude is half the battle.

2

Plans Have Changed, No Holidays Off

I received a call from my surgeon's office and my lumpectomy was scheduled for December 20. I was instructed to call the hospital as once again a lot of information was needed to pave the way for this next procedure. I called my supervisor as well to let her know about the scheduled surgery date.

I still could not believe I would be off both holidays as this was the first time since I started my nursing career for this to happen. I gave birth to each of my two sons in the spring and maternity leave certainly did not extend through these holidays. I decided this was a nice positive to focus on.

Of course, the phrase "best laid plans" came to mind when I received a call the morning of December 20 with the news that my surgeon had the flu, held off as long as possible to cancel me, but since she was not able to stand, doing surgery was totally out of the question. It would be rescheduled after the New Year, and the nurse assured me that it was not a problem delaying the surgery for two weeks.

My first call was to my husband. I tried to be funny and say "guess what, I don't think I will be off for both holidays". The joke was lost on him and details were in order. The next call was to Brian and Kathy, and I left messages about the cancellation of the surgery with the request to pass this on to the rest of the family in Massachusetts. Kathy called back and besides feeling so bad for me she also mentioned that Brian was planning to come down to be with my husband while I was in surgery. This was a total surprise and I was very touched by the gesture. Brian is a man of few words, but always there when you need him and this time was no different. I called my husband again and he felt, given the cancelled surgery and possible upcoming snow, it was better for Brian to stay put in Massachusetts. Next phone call was from Brian with the message that he was still coming down. "Brian" I said, "the surgery is cancelled, and it might snow". His response, "I am coming, you need me!" He was so right! After calling my supervisor with the new surgery date, and lying on the couch for a while wallowing in some misplaced self-pity, I came to the realization that Brian would be arriving shortly and I better take a shower and look somewhat presentable. Bob came home early from work and we went out for a nice dinner at our favorite local restaurant. The greatest blessings often come in small packages and that evening will always remain in my mind as very special one.

I guess I had the sympathy factor in place at work and had all of Christmas off. When I went to work New Year's Eve, the census was low on my floor and I was pulled to the Emergency Room to help out. At midnight I found myself next to the bed of an elderly gentleman, who was connected to many monitors, and together we watched the ball go down. I think he could think of better places to be as well, but we both made the best of it and wished each other a happy New Year with neither one of us knowing what the year would bring.

3

It is a "Go" and More

January 2, 1998

The surgery was on, no hitches this time. Bob and I arrived at the hospital early that morning and the process of being admitted started. It seemed that wherever I went I answered the same questions again and again. As a nurse, I knew this was necessary to verify the information, but I began to understand why, when I admitted a patient, there sometimes surfaced irritability for the process. I took a mental note to be even more understanding in the future having now gone through this process myself.

I was finally close to getting ready for the initial procedure of the needle localization. This was necessary for my surgeon to have a perfect guide to where the calcifications were. It was kind of nice to be in the hospital you work in as I knew many people and this somehow brought a sense of comfort. I was asked to get dressed in the famous hospital gowns, one open in the front and the other one open in the back, slippers with the skid proof bottom and to make the fashion statement complete, a paper hat. I was amazed that all were the color blue, but a different shade for each one. The technician instructed me to sit in the wheelchair, placed my chart on my lap and proceeded to tell me that she would be right back and for me not to go anywhere. I asked her where I could possibly go dressed like this and she gave me a faint smile. I guess it was too early in the day for funny questions.

The needle localization process started, and my right breast went in a vice similar as the one for my mammogram, but for a much longer duration. I received some local anesthetic and the detailed procedure to place two large needles on either side of the calcifications was initiated. It was a tedious process and the people around me were very kind and great in explaining what they were doing as I tried to tune out the fact that my breast had been flat as a pancake for quite a while now and the local anesthetic was in the process of wearing of. They finally achieved the result they needed and I was released. I made a promise to myself that I would never ever complain about the discomfort of a mammogram again as I knew now for a fact it could be much worse.

The next step was the lumpectomy. The nurse walked me into the operating room and told me that she remembered me from the time she was a student nurse in the department I worked in. "You were always very kind and helpful," she added with a smile. Having worked with so many student nurses, I could in all honesty say that I only vaguely remembered her, but I was so glad that my help and support was what she needed at that time. You just never know the impact of a simple act of kindness.

My surgeon was waiting for me, all healthy and ready to go. She checked the position of the wires, the anesthesiologist started my intravenous, said, "Good night Marianne," and I was gone. I woke up after what seemed only a few minutes, but I was sure was much longer, with a large bandage and an ice pack to the right side of my chest. According to the surgeon all went well and the office would call me when the results were in. A nice lady brought me a cup of tea and a muffin and after finishing this I was ready to go home: All and all, not too bad of a day.

The swelling persisted for a few days and the pain was very manageable with an occasional Tylenol. Two days after my surgery we were slated to go to a party at the home of the head of my husband's company. We had decided not to mention anything about the situation to anyone at his work until the results were in. Since this party was something Bob was expected to attend, and we always traveled as a pair to these types of events, I decided it would be easier if we both just went for a while to avoid Bob having to come up with some kind of excuse why I was not there. I iced the surgical area on the way down and brought a cooler with back-up ice packs for the way back. It might sound strange, but it felt good to be out and about among people, who had no idea what had happened to us these past few days, and talk about other things for a change.

4

Diagnosis

Four days later, I received the call from the surgeon's office to schedule an appointment that day with the doctor. I resisted the urge to ask what the results were as I knew full well they were not allowed to tell me.

Since the initial finding of the calcifications, I had been on this roller coaster of emotions. One day I was convinced all would be well, and then without warning, my stomach would go into knots and I had to remind myself to breathe. It was almost like I went into some kind of pre-mourning to prepare myself for what might be coming down the pike.

Bob and I were very quiet on the way to the surgeon's office. An attempt of small talk on his part fell on deaf ears and we finally pulled into the parking lot. I turned to Bob and said, "What we will hear today will change our life." Bob tried to be patient, but it had been a long week and responded with, "I cannot wait until we hear that all is well and you will be able to move on". I understood that he needed to reassure himself that I would be ok and did not come back with a snippy answer. We entered the office and I gave my name to the person behind the desk. "I am here for my results," I told her, and watched her face for some positive or negative reaction. Neither one was obvious, so either she did not know or had the best poker face ever. We took our seats and Bob started thumbing through magazines. As a newspaper person, this action always seemed to have a calming effect on him. I looked at the nurse behind the desk to see if maybe she had decided to give me the thumbs-up sign as an afterthought. No, no such luck. I looked around the room and saw another woman clutching her hands and looking very apprehensive. She had to be in the same boat as I was, and I felt so bad for her that she was all by herself. I said a quiet prayer that her results would be good. A short time later she was called in and after about 15 minutes she was back with a big smile on her face. I was so happy for her.

It was now close to 6 P.M. and it was starting to get dark outside. We were next to being called in and were guided to the surgeon's office. She was sitting behind her desk and motioned for us to take a seat at the other side. I looked at her desk and the paper with the results was upside down and I just knew. She turned the paper right side up and said, "I have good news and bad news, and will start with the bad first." You have breast cancer, but the good news is that it is stage 0, grade 3 and the margins are clear". Calmness came over me as I heard what I subconsciously had known all along, and my first question was what we were going to do about it. She did not answer as she was focusing on my husband who was ashen and had a tight grip on the arms of the chair. I told him, "Please breathe," and when my surgeon added, "she is going to be fine," the color slowly returned to his face. She continued by explaining that because the surgical area needed to heal we had to wait a few weeks before the recommended radiation treatments could be initiated.

The ride back home was initially very quiet as we were both processing the news in our own way. When we got home I headed to the phone and called my older son, Brian. I downplayed the whole situation to him, but could hear the tremendous concern in his voice as he asked the "what now" questions. Again, I decided to call my younger son, Keith, in France the next day because of the time difference. He immediately offered to come home, but I convinced him that I would be fine and looking forward to seeing him in a few short months when his year abroad would come to a conclusion and my treatments would be finished. I had to do some convincing, but he finally reluctantly agreed. Next in line were my brother and sister in law, who lived in Indiana. My sister in law started crying and my brother did not let on about his concern, asking me for many details as an older brother should, and told me that he was convinced that I would be just fine. It was not until much later, after his death, that my sister in law told me the real story. As she was walking out of their living room he told her to stop crying because I would be fine. When she had composed herself and returned a while later, she saw him standing with his face in his hands and sobbing. He knew that I needed a positive attitude from him and that was his gift to me. I also called some close friends, who were all devastated, and needed my assurance that all would be well. We gave the news to my mother-in law in person the next day and reassured her as best as we could.

The next weeks were a roller coaster of emotions. One day I was fine and then, out of nowhere, the reality of the cancer would grab me. I would wake up several times during the night sitting up straight in a cold sweat. Bob would ask, "What is the matter," and I would answer, "I have cancer," and he would hold me tight and remind me again and again that it was gone. But as much as he meant to be helpful, it was not the physical cancer, but the emotional one that had invaded my body, soul and spirit.

It was a difficult time for Bob as well. Being a man and wanted to be my protector and problem solver was just not possible and he went, what I call, into his cave. It was almost, "if we do not talk about, it did not happen". Even though I understood, it made me feel like I was on an island I did not want to be on, and it was time for drastic measures! I called our church and spoke with the person in charge of spiritual programming and told her my news. She was devastated but I told her that I would be alright; it was my husband I was worried about. I asked her to have our pastor keep an eye on him on the following Saturday morning when Bob would be attending a men's club meeting at our church. I should have known better to ask, as "keeping an eye," is not the pastor's style.

Bob came home a changed man and said, "You will not believe what happened this morning". Feeling somewhat guilty, I asked cautiously for details and he shared. After the breakfast our pastor said, "Before we go to our study and prayer time, I would like to share that Bob's wife, Marianne, has been diagnosed with breast cancer. Why don't you tell us about it Bob". God bless our pastor. He decided not to lure Bob out of his cave, but propel him out instead. Bob went on to tell me that he talked and cried and that several men hugged him and mentioned that their wives were breast cancer survivors as well and they understood the feelings of helplessness. It was a healing moment for both of us and placed us on a path that from then on we traveled together. Coincidently, I had no more middle of the night awakenings after that day.

Another special gift that month came a few days later in the form of a special friend. I was aimlessly walking through a local department store and looked at the people who were busy with their shopping. I was still so amazed how I could look so normal, be without any discomfort and have cancer. I checked if any of them did notice there was something wrong with me and decided to give me a second look. Now I was truly getting worried about my thought process and decided it was time to go home and have a cup of tea, which truly made a lot more sense. On my way to the door I bumped into a dear friend I had not seen for a while. We hugged and when she asked how everything was going I blurted out, "I have cancer". She hugged me again and wanted details. I told her that I was somewhat in limbo waiting for my treatments to start and she asked if I had plans for the upcoming weekend. When I said I did not she told me that she and two friends were going on a weekend retreat in Vermont and that there was room in the car for me to come along. She furthermore assured me that I was more than welcome to share her room. This was truly a God given blessing and everything looked so much brighter than before. I told her I was in and went home to inform Bob. He was very happy for me, especially that, since I am incredibly directionally challenged, someone else would be driving.

The retreat house was at the bottom of a mountain and the couple leading the retreat could have been the parents of many of the retreatants my age. The woman especially was so kind and, as if she knew I so needed that, several times during that weekend, just passing by, she would place her hands gently on my shoulders. It was as close as having my mom with me and God knew I needed to have that feeling of comfort.

The meals were all in silence, which is something I had never experienced, but grew to really appreciate that weekend. The weekend also included a visit to the Weston Priory where the Benedictine monks reside. We were part of a service, which was truly inspirational, and walked the grounds around the priory as dusk set in. It was a truly magical weekend and I came home renewed in every aspect.

5

Treatment Time

January 1998

Since I knew that the radiation treatments would be Monday through Friday, for a total of six weeks, I was trying to figure out how to go about working my night shift schedule around these treatments. As I was pondering this issue, I received a call from a dear friend and fellow nurse, and I told her my dilemma. She immediately told me there was no dilemma as in her words, "I had more sick time than all of them combined" and this was the time to take advantage of that. She further mentioned that if I did not listen to her she would come over to my home and knock some sense into me. I believed her and actually was so grateful for this solution that had not even entered my mind as I always reserved using my sick time when having absolutely no other choice.

27

We had another appointment with my oncology radiologist. In the admitting department, I was given the paperwork for the radiologist and I remember looking at the face sheet and there was all the pertinent information: name, address, church affiliation, doctor's name, name of person to contact in case of emergency, and the glaring diagnosis in the lower right corner: Carcinoma of the right breast. It might sound strange, but I still had this tiny hope that I would go in and the radiologist would say: "good news, lab error". Of course this did not happen, but I had renewed sympathy and much more compassion for people in denial. Since I obviously needed to move on, I asked my radiologist if she recommended that I would take time off for the duration of my treatments and she asked what floor I worked on. I mentioned the floor and added that on one side were mostly isolation rooms with serious infectious diseases. She said that if I had enough sick time it would be very beneficial for my health not to work in that environment during my radiation treatments and she was happy to sign a form to that effect for me. This was not welcome news for my supervisor, but I stood my ground as the time had come to take care of myself in the best way possible if I wanted positive results.

The next visit was mapping out the right chest area, and I assured Bob I could go solo, because I thought it was just simply laying down on the table, lines would be drawn to "mark the spot" and that would be pretty much it. Well, I was partially right but "simply' was not a part of it. For over an hour I was flat on the table, no clothes from the waist up, something I was getting used to, with my right arm, elbow bent, over my head, and strapped in a foam mold that slowly hardened around my arm. Initial pins and needles were replaced by total numbness, and I am still amazed I did not say anything. Periodically I was moved a tiny bit to the left or right and then the discussion between the technicians resumed by my feet. I could not hear what was being said and actually started to worry that maybe additional cancer was discovered and they were trying to figure out how to tell me. I knew that this thinking was not logical, but a quiet fear instilled in me and I started to try thinking about anything but the situation I found myself in. Finally, what seemed hours, the markings were made and I was released from the foam mold. A few minutes later I was standing in the dressing room with a totally numb right arm hanging beside my body, and my Dutch stubbornness was my only help in dressing myself that day.

I proceeded to go to my car with a still useless right arm and saw a package on the back seat. With all that had happened, I had forgotten that I had planned to go to the Post Office after my procedure and mail a Valentine gift to France for my son, Keith. Stubbornly, I decided that I was still going to do that and headed for the Post Office forgetting that forms had to be filled out and I was right handed. I walked up to the counter, package and forms in my left hand and tearfully asked for help. The postal employee was beyond kind, took the forms and filled out the information I provided for her. She had no idea what was going on with me, but did not question me and simply helped. I finally got home, still driving with my left hand, went into the house and kicked the first wall I saw. As I recall, that was the only time I was angry and frustrated about the whole situation. When I related the story to Bob he felt so bad he was not there for me, but I assured him that neither one of us could have expected this to be such a difficult undertaking, and that it was all good now. From that time on, I have not been by myself to any test or appointment related to cancer again, even when I tried to convince Bob I could handle it. He would look at me and state that his presence was not up for discussion, and knowing that look, I knew he meant business.

The end of January marked the start of my six weeks of radiation treatments, the last week reserved for what was called "the boost", which included increased doses to the area where the cancer had been removed.

I remember that first day well. The technician walked me into the room and I was instructed to lie on the table with my arm in the now familiar mold and under no circumstances to move any part of my body. She was very nice and told me that the treatment would only be a few minutes, 30 seconds each side, and then she would be back to bring me to the room to get dressed again. I thanked her and the next thing I knew the heavy door closed and I was all by myself. Since I was told not to move my body, my eyeballs were getting a workout. I realized that I actually signed up for receiving radiation for healing and was reminded of the people in other parts of the world who never signed up, and whose exposure to radiation had a horrible outcome. A little light went on next and this enormous machine started moving, first radiating the left side then moving over my head to do the same at the right side. I hoped this obviously heavy equipment was regularly inspected because if it ever came down on me, it was game over. I am constantly amazed about the crazy thoughts that creep into the mind when least expected. It was time to move on to more logical thinking, and since I was told that each part of the treatment would be thirty seconds, I decided to count to that number. Big mistake! I was done counting and the machine had not made any intention to make the trip to the other side in need of radiation. A new plan was in order and first I was thinking about the video game "Pac Man" where little figures have the ability to snap up anything in their way, but then decided that angels, flying around and fluttering away all the residues of cancer, was a better fit for me. The music in the room was always pleasant and I sometimes hummed along with a familiar song.

The daily treatments became a safe place to go to, a place where, for the most part, healing took place. A special friendship also developed with other daily patients and we rejoiced with each other when one of us was finished with treatments. In addition, the kindness of the nurses and technicians was overwhelming and I was always so touched how upbeat they were working in this cancer related windowless environment. Every Friday they asked what the plans for the weekend were and, without fail, on Monday asked me how my weekend was. It seemed like a little thing to do, but for me it was huge.

The treatments continued in March and thankfully my bloodwork looked good, but the tiredness and some burning of the skin was setting in. I remember going out for an early dinner with friends one night and when Bob and I returned to the car it was 8 P.M. Bob looked at me and asked where I would like to go, and I said home, I need to go to bed. This might not seem strange to some, but in our marriage that was Bob's preferred bedtime as I was the night owl in the relationship. One would think this new situation was just perfect, but going to bed early also meant I was up early, invading Bob's favorite and almost sacred early morning time. The main important issue became who would get to read the paper first and Bob solved that by ordering two papers for the remaining duration of my treatments. If all things in life could be so simple!

Since Brian and his fiancée, Kathy, were getting married in August, I decided to start looking for a dress. However, standing in the bright lights of the dressing room, my purple markings were too distracting and I decided to hold off looking for a dress until my treatments were finished.

The last week of treatments came with the expected boost treatment and I noticed that instead of being excited that I was almost done, I started having this feeling of anxiety that I could not begin to explain. Then I realized that while I was receiving the treatments I was taking action against my cancer, but after they stopped the wait and see period would begin. Once I realized the possible reason of this feeling, it somehow helped relieve some of my anxiety.

After my last treatment, Bob had planned to meet me at the hospital with a dozen pink roses, but a last minute meeting he had to attend nixed that plan and he met me at home just a short while after I got home. He felt so bad, but I was so touched by his gesture and decided to dry the roses as a remembrance of this special time. And to this day they are still standing strong!

6

Back to Work with a Detour

In the beginning of April, I was cleared by my surgeon and radiologist to return to work. I was very excited about this and looked forward to put the past few months behind me. The nurse who covered my nightshift while I was out expressed a desire to stay on that shift since it worked out better for her family, and I took her day shift, which included an occasional night shift rotation as well.

It should have been all so simple but it turned out not to be the case. My floor had merged with another one and since one of the nurses from that other floor refused to work the evening shift instead of her previous night shift, I was, without being asked, put on that evening shift with a curt note from my supervisor that it was not up for discussion. I was beyond amazed that seniority and faithful service for 28 years apparently meant nothing, and very sad this was my "welcome back" after taking time off for cancer treatments. Since the rotation to the evening shift was not conducive for my health as I was still dealing with low energy related to my radiation treatments and fading in the early evening hours, my evening rotation was changed to two twelve hour, 7 A.M. to 7 P.M., shifts, which many times were broken up into eight and four hour shifts. It felt like I was working full time instead of part time, but since this was deemed the "best solution" I decided to let it go and focus instead on being there for the patients who needed me. I had wanted to be a nurse since I was two years old and truly loved my profession. I can honestly say that there was never a time I did not want to go to work and this was the time to focus on that.

All was going well and excitement was building up about the upcoming wedding of Brian and Kathy. I bought my dress and showers were being planned. Keith returned from France and it was a great time of celebrating family and life in general.

Then in July I developed a dry cough and difficulty breathing. X-ray results showed a right upper lobe pneumonia and my medical doctor placed my on antibiotics. When there was no relief of my symptoms a repeat x-ray was ordered, and I was told by the technician that the results would be sent to my doctor. However, since this was the beginning of the week that would end with the wedding of my son, I panicked and told the technician that I had my son's wedding to attend by the end of the week and had no time to spare to make this a reality. I insisted to talk to the radiologist before I left the office and he showed me the x-ray. Even though I am a nurse, I am not very familiar with reading and interpreting x-rays, but even I knew that lobes of lungs are not supposed to look solid white. The radiologist explained that I had an increase in the pneumonia now being in my right upper lobe as well as my middle lobe, hence the increased breathing problems. I explained my wedding plight to him as well and he assured me that he would call in the results to my doctor immediately.

I drove back to her office and having already received the results she strongly suggested that I see a pulmonologist ASAP. She asked me if I had a preference and I told her whomever was available now was the winner. She called a pulmonologist known to both my husband and me and, thankfully, an appointment was available as soon as I could get there. I went back to my car, and, at this point hardly able to breath, I called Bob and told his secretary that I needed to speak with him. Bob was on the phone within seconds, and I told him something was seriously wrong and that I was going to the pulmonologist to find out what the problem was.

I don't know how Bob did it, but he was there before me, and boy was I glad to see him! The pulmonologist checked my lungs, decided to put me back on another round of antibiotics as well as prednisone to hopefully facilitate some relief of my intense shortness of breath. Since he was not sure about the cause he also planned to schedule a CAT scan and I told him that ASAP would be appreciated as I had a wedding to go to by the end of the week. He said, "We will see about that," and I said, "No, we will not, I am going one way or the other". He turned to Bob trying to get support from him but Bob just shook his head and said, "If she says she is going, she is going. You can count on that." Thankfully, there was an opening for this test within two days and on Wednesday evening of that same week, three days before the wedding, I went to the hospital for my CAT scan and then it was, once again, waiting for test results and a diagnosis.

The phrase, "the more things change, the more they stay the same," came to mind and I must admit this time I was scared about what it could possibly be. I ended up with a big purple bruise on my hand where the intravenous needed for the CAT scan dye had infiltrated, but I knew that Kathy was planning to get wrist corsages for the moms so that would no problem. Also, with all this going on I had lost about ten pounds and the dress was hanging of me. Thankfully, someone in the advertising department of Bob's work was able to locate a smaller size in a store in New Jersey, and they shipped it to the store in our area. It fitted perfectly and I was good to go for the wedding, which no matter what, I would be attending!

Thursday, two days before the wedding, Bob, my younger son Keith, and I were in the family room waiting for the phone to ring and receive the results of the CAT scan. You could cut the tension in the room with a knife. Pumpkin, our cat, walked into the room, took one look, and then walked back out, which was very telling as he always wanted to be where the family was. We were all doing our best to deal with the tenseness of waiting to hear the results of the test. Keith was behind the computer and turned around several times to give me a reassuring smile, Bob was quiet and I was sitting with my legs crossed under me just rocking back and forth. The phone rang and I picked it up. It was Brian to check if I had heard anything yet. He and Kathy were at the reception place to make sure all was in order for Saturday. I felt so bad that this mess was hanging over their heads as this should be a time of positive things. I said something to this effect to Brian, who did not want to hear any of it. I told him that we had not heard from the doctor yet and asked if he thought all would be well and this was not another cancer. He assured me that all would be well and I asked him if he felt the same prior to my breast cancer diagnosis. He said that he did not at that time, but this time he did, and somehow this worked for me.

The phone rang again and I motioned for Bob to pick it up this time. Even though this was the time before caller ID, I was sure that it was the doctor calling with results. I was right and for a while all Bob said was, "OK, OK," while I was desperately signaling the thumbs up or down sign to him. He finally gave me the thumbs up and handed me the phone. According to the pulmonologist, the CAT scan showed a serious pneumonia, but no cancer! He furthermore mentioned that he was planning to renew my antibiotic for another 10 days and told me to discontinue the prednisone. The latter part I decided to ignore until after the wedding since it had helped my breathing measurably and I did not want to take a change to have the problem return during the wedding weekend. I hung up the phone and Keith and Bob both jumped up and hugged me tightly.

The endless coughing spells, especially after taking a shower, were still present, and I had also developed a right sided costochondritis, a painful inflammation of the cartilage that connected my ribs to my breastbone. However, because of the positive news I just received this became all very minor in my book. We immediately contacted Brian and Kathy with the good news and virtual hugs were exchanged via phone as well. Time to pack suitcases and early the next morning we were on our way to Massachusetts for the August 1 wedding of Brian and Kathy.

7

Wedding Bells
And More Good Stuff

My brother and sister-in- law drove directly to Massachusetts from Indiana and we were thrilled to see each other. I had not mentioned anything to them about the whole lung problem episode, but it did not take long for them to look at me and ask what was going on. I gave a brief update and reassured them that everything was under control and I was feeling better every day. They had planned to stay with us for a week after the wedding and, knowing them as I did, I knew that they might be worried it would be too much for me to have company. The rehearsal dinner was wonderful as the weather allowed for a cookout and we enjoyed spending time with family and friends who were slowly arriving. Thanks to my continued use of prednisone, my breathing was under control and Bob and I were so grateful being able to spend this time of celebration with all of them. This week certainly ended better than the way it had started!

The next morning we woke up to beautiful sunshine and joined family and friends for a scheduled brunch at a nearby restaurant. The rest of the afternoon was spent relaxing and catching up with friends who arrived that day. One of Brian's friends arrived on a black Harley motorcycle, my all-time favorite, and Kathy, knowing this, had her picture taken by the Harley in her wedding gown. I treasure that picture as I treasure her! The wedding service started at 6 P.M. and the ceremony, just as the bride and groom, was beautiful. The reception followed and a great time was had by all. Keith enjoyed catching up with friends he had not seen for a while and I treasured the dance with my now married son. Even Bob's mom ditched her cane and danced with her grandson. It was a truly magical day!

Most of the people that had traveled out of state for this wedding decided to stay overnight, as well as Kathy's family, and we all met for breakfast the next morning. Several of our friends had teenagers at home and told them that they were definitely coming home after the wedding. They hoped that this would avoid parties to be planned, and their plan worked. I am sure many can relate to this time of trying to stay one step ahead of the very ingenious mind of teenagers.

Later that morning, Brian and Kathy left for their honeymoon and we started packing up to go back home. I was looking forward to spend the rest of the week with my brother and sister-in-law and Bob took some days off from work to join us as well.

Keith had informed us that Carrie, a friend he met in France, who was studying abroad from Scotland, was coming to visit "for only a few days". I asked, since she was coming for several weeks, where she would be going after those few days with us. There was not a definitive answer and I told Bob that she probably would be with us for the duration of her visit. I was somewhat concerned first of all, since stopping my prednisone, my breathing problems were slowly returning, and secondly, I had never met Carrie. In addition, Keith worked full time days from Monday through Friday for the summer.

Well, my fears were totally unfounded as, from the moment Carrie and I met, there was a level of comfort between us and both being European was an extra bonus! Initially, Keith would come home for lunch, but we assured him we were doing just fine and the two of us went to different places for lunch, followed by a relaxing tea in the afternoon. Having her presence turned out to be the best medicine, and several years later she joined our family as our second daughter-in-law. Since Kathy, our other daughter-in-law, several years before was supposed to come for a few days as well, but arriving with a large suitcase dispelled that notion, we have this standing joke with the girls that both of them were supposed to come for "a few days", but stayed forever in our hearts. Bob and I are truly blessed!

After Carrie left and finishing my antibiotic with no improvement noted, it was time to make another appointment with my pulmonologist. In the meantime, he had presented my case at a conference and, knowing what to look for; a repeat CAT scan finally gave the diagnoses of BOOP, which stands for bronchiolitis obliterans organizing pneumonia, a non-infectious disease, possibly related to my radiation treatments. When I came home from that visit, I did some research on the computer, but only could find information in French, which turned out not to be a problem as I had a fluent French speaking son in residence! He translated the article for me and according to that information it was definitely related to my radiation treatments. The prescribed treatment was high doses of prednisone initially, followed by decreasing doses for a total of six weeks, all of which concurred with what my pulmonologist had said.

As the previous time I was on prednisone, it worked like a charm, and I was finally cleared by my pulmonologist to return to work.

8

Downsizing as Needed

After I returned to work, I decided to make the wise decision to change my status at the hospital to per diem, which allowed me to work fewer hours. It also meant that I lost my level II status, a type of award for nurses who go above and beyond what is expected. This "award" entails much paperwork on the part of the applicant and includes documentation of proven leadership and initiative on many levels. The completed application then goes to a committee for approval.

In addition, I lost my more than 300 remaining sick hours, which I was not allowed to donate to other nurses experiencing illness, my matched retirement and insurance benefits. However, I felt there was no other choice and it was still a small price to pay for the benefit of my health. I was also very grateful to be able to maintain active as a nurse on a much less stressful level.

Also during the month of September, 1998, I received the good news that my six month follow up mammogram looked perfect, and I was good to go for another year!

In October of this year, Bob was talking to a friend, whose wife had traveled the same journey as I had, and they commiserated how often they had said the wrong thing at the right time and visa-versa. They both wished there was a support group available for the men of breast cancer survivors to provide advice how to be a support, but since there was not, they decided to create one. It was called Men to Men and met monthly in one of the rooms at the parish center of our church. Since both were business men, it was very structured with different speakers, question and answer time, and suggestions for support each month. One of the speakers was a plastic surgeon who ended up playing a very important role in our life further down the road. I still remember Bob coming home and being so impressed about this particular speaker as, in his words "he truly cares about the whole person, not just the surgical part".

I had also found an amazing support group. Initially I had started out with a well-known one, but the large number of women attending did not encourage togetherness as many women would have their own conversations during presentations. I told Bob this was not working for me and he encouraged me to go back one more time. That time closed the deal. A young woman was tearfully sharing the fact that she had been diagnosed with breast cancer and her father did not allow her to use the word "breast" in his presence. She was engaged and did not know how to tell her fiancé that she would be losing her beautiful long blond hair. I ended up shushing the women around me and was beyond stressed for her by the end of the meeting. After the meeting I verbalized my frustration to a woman sitting next to me and she shared that she felt the same way and was planning to start a support group in my home town, of all places! I told her I was in and for the next few years this much smaller group of incredible women formed an amazing bond of love and support.

Since my new work schedule was working out well and giving me extra time for other things, I decided in January of 1999 to return to college for an additional degree. Prior to going for the placement test, I dusted off one of my son's very new looking, barely used, SAT prep book and familiarized myself with mostly the English comprehension part, as being from Holland, I was not very familiar or comfortable with multiple choice. I thought this to be the best way to prepare, and I did not focus too much on the math part as I felt more comfortable about that. Again, big mistake!

I arrived at our local community college for the placement test and realized that out of all the people taking the test, only one other woman besides me was equipped with a sharpened number two pencil. We looked at each other and then realized that the test would probably be on the computer. I told her not to worry since I was sure that there would be explanations for novices like us. She seemed more reassured than I felt and decided to stay close to me. Thankfully, there was a lot of support for any questions about the use of the computer and I actually breezed thought the English comprehension questions. Empowered by that I moved on to math and was shocked to realize that I must have been asleep during the time algebra and geometry was taught during my high school years. I should have gone over the prep for this as well! Thankfully, I aced the English part, squeaked by with the math, and I had officially become a college student.

Prior to starting school, Bob and I decided on a quick flight to Indiana and surprise our nephew with our presence at his son's christening. It was also a good time to be with my brother and sister-in-law during a much better health situation to reassure the both of them that I was good to go again.

Life was moving on and I was truly enjoying being at school. There was something special about being a mature student and it being a choice for enrichment as opposed to having to do it for career sake. I had also become the go to person for the young students in my classes for accurate notes. They were always thankful for copies and amazed at the details. I was sure they did not realize that, at my age, if you do not write it down, it disappears from memory at lightning speed.

I also had resumed some community volunteer activities and started to treat myself to an occasional manicure and pedicure. Doctor visits were dwindling down to the usual, such as dentist **appointments** and regular physicals. It was all good! Bob and I participated in a Walk for the Cure event, sponsored by a breast cancer organization, for the first time and we were both very emotional reading the backs of the participant's T shirts, which mentioned names either in honor or in memory of someone. We both realized how blessed we were to be able to walk together in this celebration of life!

After graduation, Keith was able to secure a job in New Hampshire teaching at a boarding school. We loaded up a large U-Haul with furniture dating back to when we were first married, still in great condition, and started the **trip** to Keith's new abode. The elevator in the building was very small and not able to transport the large pieces of furniture to the fourth floor. I still don't know how we accomplished the job of furnishing Keith's apartment but somehow we did.

Carrie, his now official girlfriend, moved from Scotland and secured a job in Washington D.C. She would fly to New Hampshire each weekend to visit Keith and we would joke that the two of them probably were the only people of their age with frequent flyer miles.

9

Could There Be More Happenings In a Short Time?

September 1999 started out on a positive note, but that did not last very long. We finally had been able to convince my mother-in-law to wear a life alert pendant, and we were notified on a week day around eleven P.M. about her not responding after pushing the button. Bob rushed to her home, while I got dressed in the meantime. Bob had called me after he found his mom on the floor and I told him to check for a pulse. Thankfully there was one, and after the ambulance arrived, he drove back home to pick me up on the way to the hospital. My mother-in-law had experienced a massive stroke and was admitted to the Intensive Care Unit.

Mom did regain consciousness a few times, and one time was very special for my husband and two sons. Brian who lives in Massachusetts decided to call his brother in New Hampshire, with the simple message "I am going home, Dad needs us". Keith was able to get his classes covered and one hour later they were on the road. Bob came home to pick me up to go to the hospital as we had received the message that mom had regained consciousness and the breathing tube would be removed that morning. Just before we left, our two sons walked in the door and the look of grateful surprise on my husband's face was very touching. The three of them hugged tightly right in the middle of the kitchen and then we all went to the hospital. I insisted on staying with mom while her breathing tube was being removed and talked reassuringly to her while the process took place. Immediately after that Bob walked in with the kids behind him. She gave him a beautiful smile and then, realizing who was behind him, pushed him aside and gave an even broader smile to her two grandsons! We spent some time with her and encouraged her to either nod or squeeze our hand if she understood us, as talking was not so easy for her after being intubated for a while. The time came that Bob had to return to work and I went with my sons to a local diner for lunch and filled them in on all the details before both of them had to return to their respective jobs.

Mom was moved from the ICU to a floor in the hospital and, regretfully, experienced having a series of additional mini strokes, which caused her to slip back into her prior semi-comatose state. Our life revolved around visits to the hospital, where more often than not, I would give her the personal care that was not provided for her by some of the nurse's aides on duty. Bob could not believe the condition in which we would sometimes find his mom and was planning to file a complaint, but I told him to leave it alone as she, because of her semi-comatose state, would not be able to tell us if there were retributions to that action. As a nurse for many decades, I had seen it all!

Mom regained a very short period of consciousness while I was washing her about one week later. She looked straight at me and thanked me for being so good to her, and I told her to hang in as there was more to come. She nodded, closed her eyes, and never spoke again.

Bob also had a special connection with his mom during this time. He went to visit her and was told that his mother had gone for a CAT scan to assess the amount of damage done by the recent mini strokes. The nurse told him that mom had been gone for about an hour and should be back soon. When soon did not happen within the next half hour, he called me and asked my opinion. Again knowing what I know, I told him that she probably was in a hallway somewhere near the CAT lab waiting for an orderly to bring her back. I suggested he ask where the CAT lab was and go there to find out what the delay was. He did, and just as I suspected, his mom was strapped on a stretcher all by herself in a hallway. He loudly demanded action to bring his mother back or he would take care of it himself. It was at this time his mom opened her eyes and gave him the thumbs up sign. Priceless!

According to the results of the test there was little to no hope of recovery, and the difficult decision had to be made to move mom to a nursing home for the final weeks of her life.

One would think that this was enough for one month, but that was not to be.

10

Yes, There Can Be More!

My one year follow up mammogram scheduled for September showed calcifications in two different areas of the same breast, and the journey, which started sixteen months ago, resumed once again.

I met with my surgeon and a tactile biopsy was scheduled. For those not familiar with this procedure, let me tell you it was quite an experience. I was placed on my stomach on a hard table, with the affected breast hanging down through a hole. The other breast, wanting no part of this, was pushed and pulled to the side as it started to actually wonder who had the better deal. The one hanging down was now placed in the all too familiar vice and, after locating the calcifications, biopsies were performed and clips placed for biopsy site identification. Again, it was a lengthy procedure and the main discomfort was my neck, which I was allowed to turn from side to side to release the tension that was building up in that area. The test was finally done and I was released from the table. I felt a little dizzy and almost fell from the stool I was sitting on. The nurse caught me and I told her that it would be a sad thing to tell my husband that the test went well, but unfortunately I fell off the stool and broke my hip. We both laughed, and once again I was so grateful for the kind and caring people I kept encountering during these un-planned events in my life.

I received the expected call from the office with an appointment time of late in the afternoon. Since I now knew what that meant, I told the receptionist that, given the already stressful time we were experiencing concerning our mom, I was not willing to wait until then to find out the results. My surgeon came to the phone and told me that it was cancer again, which I already knew, and that one of the tumors was invasive this time, which I did not expect. Bob hugged me tight and said tearfully how bad he felt for me to have to go through this again. I hugged him back and assured him that this was a bump in the road and we were going to tackle this situation just we had done with other ones in our life.

On the way to our appointment, we received a call from the nursing home. Mom was experiencing some difficulty breathing and we were asked what hospital we would like her to be brought to. I told them to put her on oxygen and that we would be there within the hour to evaluate the situation. Since Mom had a living will stating her desire for no extra-ordinary measures, I felt comfortable doing so. Bob asked if we should call back and have mom go to the hospital anyway, but I told him that we had to accept the fact that more than likely she was not going to get better, and in her current state to be brought via ambulance to the hospital, be poked and prodded again, would be so scary for her. In addition, her current immune system was so low that a secondary problem, such as an infection, was likely and cause more pain and suffering for her. I furthermore reminded him that the care givers in the nursing home she was in could not be kinder or more compassionate, which was a much appreciated change from our previous experience. Bob took a deep breath and agreed with me.

We arrived at the surgeon's office and went over the details of this latest cancer. I was armed with information because, immediately following my treatments for my initial cancer, I had done my research just in case this cancer would return. The information I gathered was that this time it would be a mastectomy, possible chemo and the recommended reconstruction, because of my radiated skin, would be a tram flap, which uses your own tissue. I had printed this out, stored it in a safe place and not told anyone about it. Good thing I had done this in a much calmer time and it was now time to share this information with my surgeon for implementation of plan B.

Who knew we would go further down the alphabet to plan C! My surgeon agreed with all the information I had gathered, but then told me that, since the sentinel node procedure was not yet performed in any of the area hospitals, she wanted me to go to one that did.

She explained that a sentinel lymph node is the first lymph node to which cancer cells are most likely to spread from a primary tumor, and a sentinel lymph node biopsy can be used to help determine the extent, or stage, of cancer in the body. She furthermore mentioned that because this procedure involved less extensive surgery and the removal of fewer lymph nodes than standard lymph node surgery, the potential for adverse effects or lymphedema is lower. A negative result suggested that the cancer had not developed the ability to spread to nearby lymph nodes or other organs, and a positive one indicated that cancer was present in the sentinel lymph node and might be present in other nearby lymph nodes and, possibly, other organs. This information could help a doctor determine the stage of the cancer and develop an appropriate treatment plan. She gave some additional details about the procedure and reinforced the most important part that it would avoid removing fifteen or more nodes, which was the procedure at that time.

Despite all that logical information, I was devastated she would not be doing the surgery as that was so high on my comfort level. She understood, but said that if the roles were reversed, I would tell her the same thing. She convinced me by saying that she did not want to take out that many nodes, find out they were all negative for cancer, and increase the possibility for lymphedema, a permanent swollen arm. She recommended a doctor in the other hospital and suggested we call for an appointment. I felt like a lost puppy and must have looked it because she came from behind her desk and hugged me.

Next it was time to go to the nursing home to check on mom's declining health status, and, thankfully, we had made the right decision as mom's breathing had improved and she was resting peacefully.

When we arrived home, I made the usual calls to family and friends. As always, my first call was to Brian, who was devastated and concerned about the major surgery I had to undergo. However, I had decided to come up with the mantra, "I am not having a mastectomy, but a tummy tuck covered by insurance". It was quiet at the other end and then Brian said "If you are going to be so darn positive about this, it will be hard for me to be bummed out". I responded "There you go positive thoughts helpful and appreciated". Next call was to Keith, who was equally upset as Brian and wanted details as that was helpful for him to deal with this unexpected turn in our life. I called several of my close friends with the same mantra and added that the fat moved from my stomach was going to look a lot better in its new location. One of my friends asked if I would need chemo and I told her that we would not know until after the surgery and the lab results were in. But if I did I would be looking forward to no bad hair days during the upcoming holiday season and get myself the best wig available! I had made the decision that all would be well, and that was the only thing I would be concentrating on.

11

Friends with Connections, Saying Goodbye to Mom

The next morning it was time to call the doctor recommended by my surgeon and make an appointment. I was still in my pajamas and Bob in a suit, as he was planning to go to work after the call had been made, since neither one of us was expecting an appointment being available for that day. Little did we know that there would be none available for the next six weeks! Bob made that appointment and then put the phone down. I was so shocked that initially I could not even speak, and I finally mastered to say that, since one of my tumors was invasive, that was too long of a time to wait. Needless to say, all the positive thoughts from the night before were flying right out of the window.

We both sat at the kitchen table in total silence for a while, not knowing what to do next as this was a whole new scenario for us. Then Bob had a lightbulb moment as he recalled our presence at a party where we met two incredible ladies. One was a breast cancer survivor and because of her negative experiences during her diagnosis and treatments decided that she, even while currently in Stage 4 breast cancer, was going to be instrumental in creating an all comprehensive center for women diagnosed with breast cancer. She was in the process of securing financial backing, and the person with her was a nurse, who would play a very important part in this vision of hers. As we had a common thread, I spent most of my time with my co-survivor, while Bob asked many detailed questions of the nurse. They exchanged business cards and Bob told her that he thought the creation of this type on center was a great idea and to let him know if there was anything he could do from his end to speed the process along. Little did we know that the help would first come from their end instead.

Bob found the business card, placed the call and told the nurse about the situation. She told him to sit tight and that she would call him back shortly. Ten minutes later we received a call from the other person we met that evening who was on her way to Maine for a conference. She asked when I would like an appointment, and since it would be a mastectomy, did I want reconstruction, and if so, by whom. I was flabbergasted with this amazing, wonderful turn of events and mentioned that whenever she could get an appointment it would be fine and gave her the name of the plastic surgeon Bob had met as a speaker during the time of the men's support group.

She called back within a half hour. I had an appointment for the upcoming Wednesday with the new surgeon, and another one with the plastic surgeon on Thursday, all in this same week! I thanked her profusely, but she simply said it should be this easy for all women and the main reason that she, despite her diagnosis, was working so hard to make this a reality and give women a safe place to go during an incredibly difficult time of their life.

Bob and I looked at each other and still could not believe how every thing looked so much brighter than a little over a half hour ago. I told him that he should call the kids and update them and then go to work, and I would take a shower and go to class and then the nursing home to visit mom. I called both doctor's offices and gave them my cell phone number so I could be reached if there were pre-appointment calls from the new surgeon or plastic surgeon.

I still remember standing in the shower and being so at peace in the middle of this storm. In essence, nothing had changed, and at the same time everything had because two caring women took a big concern of our shoulders and then took care of it, allowing Bob and I to resume our positive attitude and battle, once again, this uninvited and unwelcome guest in our life.

The rest of the day was kind of surreal. I went to class, met with my professor afterward and informed him that I had to go for major surgery and that I would have to be out of class for about 3 weeks. I suggested that it would be best to drop the class, but he disagreed. He stated that since I was an A student, I would be able to catch up without any problems. We agreed that as soon as I was home after the surgery, Bob would be able to pick up class notes and he would be in contact with me via email for all other matters. This was exciting news for me as I really enjoyed this particular class. I updated Bob later about this unexpected chain of events and told him that I might be losing a breast, but I would not lose my three credits! Bob just looked at me, shook his head, and said, "Only you would see this as a positive".

After class I visited mom and, since I had formed a close relationship with the immediate staff taking care of her, I decided to inform them about my diagnosis. Being a constant fixture at mom's bedside in the nursing home, I wanted them to know that if I was not there, it probably was because of the preparations for the surgery. I asked them not to talk about this around mom as I knew that, even being comatose, the hearing was still present. Mom was very devastated when I was diagnosed the first time around and was convinced that it would never happen again. I knew it would be beyond stressful to hear about the current one and not be able to communicate.

After dinner that evening I was truly emotionally drained and decided that "day was done" and went upstairs to bed with the hope of getting a good night sleep before the appointments of the next day. Just as I was dozing off, I heard the phone ring and then Bob coming upstairs. He mentioned that the phone call was from our pastor who would like us to come to church the next morning for an anointing. Since the time was way before my appointment I agreed and went back to sleep.

Having never been anointed before, I had no idea what to expect. First there was the regular, though shortened, Mass with about forty people present. Afterward, our pastor asked me to come forward and I sat down on a chair provided for me. To my amazement all the people present, who I did not know, stayed and stood close by. The pastor shared my diagnosis with them and asked me to talk about it. I remember saying that I was not angry about this new diagnosis, but felt very bad for my family having to go through all this with me once again. The people stretched out their hands to me in prayerful support as the pastor anointed my forehead and my palms with oil from Israel. He apologized when a small drop fell on my slacks, but I told him not to worry. Next he went to Bob and stated that he needed to be anointed as well as the two most important women in his life were being attacked, and the same outstretched hands of prayerful support were now directed towards him. The pastor then said, "This is our prayer for you:"

Be at peace

Do not look forward to what might happen tomorrow

The same everlasting Father who cares for you today will take care of you tomorrow and every day

Either He will shield you from suffering, or He will give you unfailing strength to bear it

Be at peace then and put aside all anxious thoughts and imaginations.

The prayer was on a small card and given to Bob and me. We in turn have shared this special prayer with many others going through a difficult time.

The anointing was a truly sacred time for both of us and God's peace, which is truly beyond human understanding, filled our hearts and minds. Afterward several people came up to us with words of encouragement and one elderly man gave me his late wife's favorite medal and said he would pray every day for me. Bob and I walked out of the church, looked at each other and I said, "So, I am going for surgery, big deal" and we both started laughing. This amazing outpouring of kindness and compassion had changed everything.

We were in the office of the new surgeon and, sitting on the table waiting for her to come in, I looked down and saw the oil stain on my slacks. I cupped my hand over it and smiled as I recalled the amazing experience of the early morning anointing. My surgeon walked in and my fears about starting with an unfamiliar doctor were immediately put to rest. She was kind, very reassuring and agreeing with my choice of a tram flap reconstruction she went into some details of that particular surgery. She also knew that we were scheduled to see the plastic surgeon the next day and said that as soon as she could coordinate a date with him for surgery, her office would give us a call.

Bob decided, since we were in an area of many fine restaurants, he was treating me to lunch, and it was during lunch that Bob brought up the reconstruction part of the surgery. Since I had researched the procedure, and being a nurse, it obviously did not affect me hearing the details as they apparently had affected him. He was mostly concerned about the long time under anesthesia and reassured me that he did not care if I had the reconstruction because he loved me in any shape or form. I realized he was concerned about the fact he might lose me and I knew I had to tread lightly. I told him I was touched by his love for me, but this was something I did for myself, as not doing so would be a constant reminder of the cancer for me and hinder my ability to move on. He understood, but I could tell he was still very worried.

The next day was my appointment with my plastic surgeon, and it was like old home week for him and Bob as this was the surgeon who spoke at the Men to Men support group and the one Bob was so impressed with at that time. I could tell that Bob was feeling more comfortable about my decision as he had full faith in the abilities of this surgeon. Once again I was in my now familiar uniform of no clothes above the waist and to add to the picture, this time my stomach was exposed as well. The surgeon checked the amount of skin and fat in my abdomen and compared it with was needed for the reconstruction. He looked at me with a big smile and told me it was very doable. I probably should have been insulted, but that part of my body was never my greatest asset. He furthermore told me that half of my abdominal muscle would be taken for the reconstruction and that sit-ups would no longer be a possibility after that. I laughed and asked if it looked that that was something my stomach was used to. He was kind and just smiled. Now the waiting time for the date of the surgery began.

I **spent my** time between going to class and the nursing home. Bob would drop me off at school and then pick me up after class and then we would both go to visit mom. I would stay at her bedside doing my homework and Bob would pick me up again after work, which enabled him to visit again for a while.

On Friday, October 8, we finally received the phone call we were waiting for. I was scheduled to undergo a preliminary procedure by my plastic surgeon to prepare the abdominal flap for surgery. I mentioned to mom's caregivers that I would not be there that day and possibly the next one. However, the morning of the surgery I received a call from one of my favorite nurses that mom had passed away. I called Bob and then the hospital to let them know that under the circumstances I might be a little late for my appointment. Thankfully, the people I spoke with were kind and understanding. A short time later I heard the front door open and there was Bob, just standing there with a grief-stricken expression on his face. I went over to him and we just held each other for quite a while as that was the only thing that made sense.

Bob was able to compose himself and realized that we were going to be late for my preliminary surgery. I reassured him that the hospital was aware and we were given some leeway regarding the scheduled time. We were very quiet on our way to the hospital as we were both, each in our own way, trying to deal with the loss of mom. Sometimes when things are so big, the only solution is to be still as you try to process sad events.

We arrived at the hospital and were greeted with kindness and compassion by a staff who felt so bad for us. After the now very familiar admitting questions were completed, I gave Bob a hug and was taken to the operating room. The initial idea was that I would receive general anesthesia, but since I had never experienced that and not sure how I would react I asked the nurse if intravenous sedation could be substituted instead. She said she did not think so but to ask the anesthesiologist. I told him that my mother-in-law had passed away that morning and that tomorrow I needed to go with my husband to the nursing home and the funeral home, which was something I definitely did not want Bob to have to do all by himself.

The anesthesiologist understood, but could not make that decision without my surgeon's consent, but he also did not think intravenous sedation would be a possibility for this procedure. I suggested we should wait for my surgeon before proceeding and he agreed. When my surgeon arrived I discussed the situation with him and we decided on local anesthesia first to make the incision and some preliminary work, and then give me intravenous sedation to complete the procedure. He had never done it like this before, but he was pretty sure that would work and that was good enough for me.

It all worked our perfectly and after a few hours I was discharged with post op instructions and we were on our way home. I decided to lie on the couch and rest, while Bob started making calls to our children with the sad news about their grandmother's passing and the good news that the preliminary surgery went well. The next difficult calls for him were to the nursing home and the funeral home to make an appointment for the next day regarding the wake and funeral arrangements. Thankfully, the owners of the funeral home were people Bob had known most of his life and also knew his mom, which made it more personal and somehow a little easier.

Regretfully, I did not get the good night sleep I was hoping for because the sandwich I ate for dinner, thinking it would count as a light one, was a big mistake. I ended up dealing with nausea and vomiting most of the night and not able to take the prescribed pain medication. I spend the night sitting on the couch with an ice bag to the surgical site, which provided some relief, as I seriously questioned my decision making process. Lesson learned if there was ever a next time!

The next morning Bob stressed to me that, given my lack of sleep, he thought it would be wise for me to stay home. I convinced him that I would be fine, stay in the car and sit down whenever the situation allowed. He reluctantly agreed.

Our first stop was at the flower shop to get an arrangement for the staff who had been mom's care takers. As promised, I stayed in the car for this. We arrived at the nursing home and were embraced by the incredible people who had been such a special part of our life during a difficult time. I stayed in the supervisor's office while Bob signed the necessary papers and collected the family pictures that had been in mom's room. I had brought these in, including a beautiful one of mom at the wedding of Brian and Kathy. During my time as a nurse, I found it to be helpful for me and other caretakers to see the person before they became ill. It attested to the fact that there was more to this person in the bed besides their illness, and also gave the opportunity for family members to share this with the staff taking care of their loved ones.

Our next stop was the funeral home and it did not take long for the arrangements to be made. The wake was scheduled for Sunday, but because of Monday being a national holiday the burial had to be delayed until Tuesday. We returned home and I took a long nap, catching up on much needed rest. Bob called the kids with these updates and later that day, Brian, Kathy, Keith and Carrie arrived at our home.

It was so wonderful to have all of them around us as we had been a "two man show" until then. The guys hugged me and then spent some quality time with their father, and the girls made sure I did not overdo it and were a tremendous help taking care of any necessary details regarding the wake and plans for after the burial. Whatever they decided on was fine by me as it was such a wonderful, relaxing feeling not to have any responsibilities and decision making for a while. I emailed my professor that, because of the funeral, I would not be in class on Tuesday to take the midterm, and he emailed me back with his sympathy for our loss.

The wake was well attended by family and friends, but one attendee was most special for my husband. Bob has two very **exceptional** friends who have known each other since childhood. They have always been there for each other in good times and bad and even though one of these friends lived quite a distance away, it did not stop him from driving many hours to being able to attend the wake. When he walked in, Bob had trouble holding back his emotions as they hugged each other. There is no greater treasure that a true friend!

That evening I shared with the girls that I was planning to give a eulogy for mom. First they were concerned that it might be too much for me after the surgery, but after I told them that at one time I had promised mom to do that, Kathy suggested I share it with them. We huddled in the kitchen as I read an outline that I had created to which I added some additional thoughts. Both girls thought it was a wonderful dedication and Kathy suggested to add the part when Brian and Keith visited their grandmother in the hospital and how much joy that had given her. That was a great suggestion and I thanked both of them for their support. At one point during this collaboration time Brian walked into the kitchen to get something out of the refrigerator, paused for a moment, and then smiled at me. I know he felt like

I did. Despite the circumstances, this time was somehow peaceful and comforting for all of us, and added to the special bond we already had as a family. It was time to go to bed with hopefully less problems than the night before. I hugged and thanked all of them and had the best sleep.

The funeral was two days later and I was a little nervous about my ability to do the eulogy. In addition, I had to use a hand microphone and was wondering how I was going to handle that and my index cards. I shared this with one of the pastors at mom's church and he took me aside and shared a beautiful prayer of encouragement with me. I was good to go.

I walked up to the podium and started sharing the story about my relationship with mom. It had been, like most things in life, a journey. We were very different people, me the "everything is possible optimist" and mom not so much, and we started out having our love for her son and my husband as the only thing we had in common. But that was a great start and over time increased to mutual love and respect for each other. We became even closer in our relationship after Bob's father passed away, which was so devastating for her as well as for our family. After a prolonged period of sadness and support from Bob, me and other family and church members she slowly became more independent and willing to venture out.   We signed her up for a senior bus that picked her up at her home and she made some new friends while attending the senior center. Since taking the bus for grocery shopping was stressful for her because she would rush in fear of the bus leaving, I decided that we would have a weekly "date" for that. I would pick her up and we would always go for lunch first. Besides going to local diners, Mom also loved Italian food and I would try to find a new place to try out and then we would compare it to the previous one. This was always stressful for Bob, because both his mother and I were seriously directionally challenged and he would just wait for the call to let him know we were lost. I must say we surprised him many times by finding the place all by ourselves! At these lunches mom shared a lot of details from her life from the time she was a young girl and I really got to know her and understood why we were so different and how blessed we were to be given this extra time to bond. For some reason, we were talking about eulogies one time and I told her that I would do that for her. She asked what was there possibly to say about an old cook like her, and I laughed and said, "Plenty, and all good".

Afterwards, we would do our grocery shopping and I would always tell her to take her time. Many times I would see her in one of the isles reading labels in order to make a decision about what to buy and enjoying the time to do so. She was on this positive track for several years, but always terribly missed her Henry and that started to show more in the last year of her life. When we were driving to the nursing home the Saturday after she passed all I could think was that she was with her beloved Henry, both without illnesses that had plagued their lives toward the end. This thought gave me such great peace and joy.

I ended my eulogy by telling the audience that mom never cared about material things and was in the habit that if you liked something in her home, it would be in a bag and handed to you in a split second. I continued by sharing that mom however did deeply care about people getting along, especially if it concerned family members. I then asked the people present in the church to look around in their life for any broken relationships, and, in mom's memory, make the first step to healing that relationship. Several people contacted me afterward and said that I had motivated them to do just that.

Later that day we returned home and after spending some more time together with just the six of us, it was time for everyone to return to their other obligations. I had spoken to Brian previously about my scheduled surgery date the following week and before I even had to ask he said he already told his boss he needed that time off and would be there. Deep down I knew all would be well, but just in case it was not, I did not want Bob to be by himself.

The next day I was scheduled for a visit to the anesthesiologist for my impending surgery. Bob and I were sitting in his office and Bob said something funny and we both started laughing. At that time the anesthesiologist walked in and asked if I was the patient. I told him I was because I did not think my husband wanted to be one and he said that, with that positive attitude, I was going to be just fine. He did follow that encouraging statement with a detailed examination, and told me I was good to go.

Before my surgery I received wonderful letters and cards from the members of my new support group. Ironically, just a week prior to my diagnosis, I was with this group and since one member was thinking about reconstruction, two other members decided to have a "show and tell". I came home and shared with Bob how amazing these tram flap reconstructions looked, not knowing at that time it would even convince me more to undergo this procedure when I was diagnosed for the second time.

Also in the mail came a very special letter from a church member, who was diagnosed with breast cancer many years ago. I was still working the night shift and she was assigned to me. I did not connect the name with the face until I went to take her vital signs. She grabbed my hand and told me she was so scared she would not be able to see her sons grow up. I reassured her and she asked me to pray for her. I answered affirmative, but when I was leaving her room I heard this voice which said, "She does not need you to pray for her, but with her". Knowing that voice I answered "You know that is not something I am comfortable with" and the answer was "I gave you the blue book". I had discovered this blue booklet the night before on the table in the nurse's station and started flipping through it. It was filled with short prayers for all occasions and I remember thinking what a great idea that was. Little did I know that God was preparing me to get out of my comfort zone to be a support for someone in need of that. I walked to the nurse's station with the desperate hope it would not be there, but there it was in all its glory! I nervously looked through it and came upon one of my favorite verses from Philippians 4:6 and 7 which reads "Do not be anxious about anything, but in every situation, by prayer and petition, with thanksgiving, present your requests to God. And the peace of God, which transcends all understanding, will guard your hearts and your minds in Christ Jesus". Armed with my little blue book I went back into the room, where my patient was still wide awake and anxious. I told her that God had put on my heart to share His words with her and I did. She fell in a deep sleep immediately after and thanked me in the morning for my gift to her.

Somehow she had heard about my diagnosis and wrote me the most beautiful letter. What touched me most was the part that she would pray that an angel like me would come into my room at night and give me the same peace I had given her. Her prayer for me was answered big time and mine for her as well as she has been blessed by not only seeing her sons graduate from high school and college, but still being here to enjoy much more.

I returned to class the next day and found out that several other students had not taken the midterm either and my professor was offering a makeup date the next Monday. He asked who would be able to be there and I raised my hand. Knowing that my surgery was Tuesday, the next day, he told me that I would be able to make the midterm up at another time. I went to him after class and shared that I had never gone under general anesthesia and did not know what it would do to my brain and all the knowledge that had been stored about this class. It all made perfect sense to me, but he shook his head and told me that I was stressing him out. I told him I would be there with the others on Monday and left him still shaking his head.

My decision to take the midterm on Monday worked out perfect. I studied most of the weekend, which kept my mind busy in a positive way, and since Sunday was a beautiful day weather-wise, Bob and I enjoyed a nice Sunday afternoon drive after church and went out for lunch. We also stopped at a store where I loaded up on toiletries and other items to take with me to the hospital.

I went to class the next day and was surprised to see that I was the only one showing up for this test. My professor gave me the paperwork for the test and said that he just knew I would show up. I just smiled and went to the assigned cubicle to take my midterm. I found out after my surgery via email from my professor that I had scored a 98 on the test. More power to mature students!

On that same Monday, I was scheduled for the sentinel node procedure in the afternoon. This procedure is usually performed just prior to surgery, but my new surgeon was concerned that my radiated breast tissue might slow down the process of the dye going to the nodes and suggested I should come the day before. She was hoping this would work, but was not able to give any guaranties.

Bob and I teamed up again, fully expecting a simple procedure, which it could have been but definitely was not. Being in a teaching hospital, I knew that students would be given the opportunity to give it a try and I was right. I was back in the vice, given some local anesthetic, and the probing began. The first two tries were not successful and I started to get nauseous. By now I had come to a point in my life of speaking up when needed and calmly informed the doctor instructing the students that the next time would be done by someone who knew what they were doing. I also informed her that the local anesthesia had worn off and I would greatly appreciate a refill before proceeding. Thankfully the doctor agreed and within a short amount of time the area to be injected was located, and the dye injected felt like solid steel entering my body. After that I was released and allowed to go on my merry way.

I walked out and Bob, fully expecting a jolly Marianne was deeply disappointed. I told him this was a horrible experience and I did not want to talk about it at the moment. We walked quietly out of the hospital, but by the time we got to the car I had regained my bearings. I reminded him to stop at a particular department store, but he suggested that it might be better if we went straight home. I told him that this was the last day of a special sale to "buy one pair of shoes and get one pair free" at my favorite department store, and since that would be the only positive after the procedure, we were going for it. They turned out to be very nice shoes and I was happy with the great deal.

12

Round 2 Against Cancer!

Brian arrived early Monday evening as promised and tension, as well as fear, was building in Bob about the impending surgery scheduled for the next day. We made small talk for most of the evening and then we all turned in early. So much had happened these past few weeks that **thoughts about** this surgery had been placed on the back burner, only to return in full force.

I was the last one to go to bed and while in the bathroom taking of my make-up it came to me that there should be a small, private goodbye ceremony as well as a heads up for the breast, which was leaving me the next day. I stood in front of the mirror and viewing the delinquent part of my body I shook my head. The whole area was filled with needle marks and bruises and it was truly a very sad sight. I calmly explained that I had gone above and beyond all efforts to save her, but she just wouldn't listen and the time had come for her to go. I said I was sorry, but the decision had been made. I turned off the light and actually had a restful sleep that night.

The next morning we were all in the kitchen and to break the obvious tension I asked Bob if he wanted to say a prayer. He said yes, but was only able to get halfway through and my heart was hurting for him. When Bob left the kitchen, I noticed Brian looking at me with the same worry and I said, "Well, beside class, I had nothing planned for today, how about you?" And taking my lead he responded that, besides work, it was the same for him. I concluded that in that case we were good to go and we were on our way. Bob and I drove together and Brian followed in his car as he was planning to go back home when the surgery was over and after making sure I was all right. As in previous trips for tests and surgeries, it was quiet in the car. Halfway to the hospital I noticed a bill board featuring a mother, daughter and grandchild and the phrase "Because of advanced technology in the fight against breast cancer I am here to enjoy my grandchildren". We both looked and I said, "that is kind of encouraging, isn't it?' Bob took my hand and said, "Absolutely". Little did we know that we would be blessed years later with a granddaughter and a grandson, who make us laugh and have become the joy of our life.

We arrived at the hospital and the usual answering of questions was followed by the blue dress-up experience so well known to me by now. After a visit by the anesthesiologist and my surgeon, and hugs and kisses from my guys, I was wheeled to a hall way, lined up like a train car with other people on stretchers. My anesthesiologist began looking for a vein to start my intravenous, which is not as easy as it sounds because I have lousy veins. Being a typical nurse, and in addition having gone through this before, I gave some suggestions, and he, to his credit, was very gracious about that. While we were waiting for the operating room to be ready we heard "Laska, anyone by the name Laska" and I turned to him and mentioned that this was probably not followed by "table for two". He laughed and agreed with me. We motioned to the person with the question where our location in the lineup was, and were told that the plastic surgeon wanted to see me prior to surgery because he had to mark the surgical site. We were taken out of the line-up and I insisted that we would not go past the window of the waiting room as that would cause undue stress for my family. My by now new best friend, the anesthesiologist, said he knew another way and we ended up on an adventuress trip through the catacombs of the hospital. You just cannot make this up!

I was wheeled into a cubicle where my plastic surgeon was waiting and, after apologizing for the situation, he asked me to stand next to the stretcher. In doing so my hospital gown slipped off my shoulder and was fast on its way down to the floor. My surgeon was not aware as his total focus was on making blue magic marker lines on my breast, which would be going away, and my abdomen, which would serve as a wonderful replacement. The happening did not go unnoticed by the anesthesiologist, who caught the gown half way down my back and gently placed it back on my shoulders, securing it with both hands. It was such a simple gesture and at the same time so huge as it was filled with kindness and respect for me as a person. I looked down at the markings and asked my surgeon if he should mark "do not remove" on the other breast, but he assured me that he knew what he was doing and not to worry.

Back on the stretcher, back the way we came, and at this time the OR was ready for me. I remember how cold it was in there and started shivering. The next thing I knew a warm blanket was placed over me and tucked around my body, something like a parent would do for their child. It was very comforting.

The anesthesiologist mentioned to all in attendance that he had a joke and I told him it had to be a clean one and he said, "Of course". But before he could start, the surgeon who would perform the mastectomy walked in with a surgical intern and asked for my permission for that intern to observe. I said, "Absolutely". She then asked how I was doing and I told her I was doing well but that my husband was having a difficult time. I shared with her that I thought he was worried that I might die, but that she and I knew better. She smiled and said she was going to wait until I was asleep and, since she could not start until the radiologist had checked on the results of the sentinel node procedure done the day before, she would go to the waiting room to reassure Bob. The last thing I remembered is her gently stroking my arm and I was asleep.

I woke up and was informed that all had gone well with the surgery and I was now in the recovery room. My nurse asked if I was in pain and I told her "no, just very nauseous." She told me she could take care of that, gave me some intravenous medication and I drifted off to sleep again. The next time I woke up she was right there and mentioned that I was already off the stretcher and in my bed, which I appreciated beyond measure. People having gone through surgery can identify with that as trying to move from a stretcher into a bed after any kind of surgery is a painful challenge. As a nurse I always felt so bad for my patients and tried to help make the transition as smooth as possible for them.

I was finally deemed awake and stable enough to be discharged from the recovery room and going through the hallway back to my room two familiar faces appeared at either side of my bed in the form of broad smiling Bob and Brian. They both had their hand on my shoulder, walking alongside the bed while Bob was updating me on the good news both surgeons had given them. They finally had to let go because the doorway was not wide enough for my entourage. The nurse plugged in my bed, took my vital signs and explained the mechanics of the bed as well as how to use my pain medication via a push of a button.

The three of us talked for a while, but because I was getting sleepy, Bob and Brian decided to leave and let me rest. Brian had a long drive back home and Bob would be back early the next morning. They both bent over the bed and kissed me good night, and before Bob left I asked him to move my tray table with the phone closer by. He asked why I needed the phone, but I told him just to do it. It probably went back to the times that the phone would be ringing in a patient's room and, since they could not reach it, and did not have their call light within reach either, were understandably totally stressed out by the time I came into the room. It became my mission to always check before leaving a patient's room and making sure that phones and call lights were within their reach.

It turned out to be the right thing to ask for. After waking up in a now dark room I reached for my light button in the bedrail, but it would not go on. I tried to call the nurse, but that was not happening either. I obviously had a bed without any power and at first I did not know what to do. Then I remembered the phone! I grabbed all my tubes on the left side of me and slowly moved my body to the right in the direction of the phone. I finally reached the receiver and dialed 0 for operator, who asked how she could help me. I told her my name and room number and that I would like to see a nurse. I am sure she was wondering about my mental state, but kindly explained that just simply pushing the button in my bedrail would accomplish that. I replied that I understood, but my bed was dead, and would she please call the nurses station for me. After a silence, she said she would and before I knew it several nurses ran into my room, which made me wonder what she had told them. It turned out that in the process of saying goodnight and leaning into the bed, my guys had moved the bed just enough to partially unplug it, which was an easy fix for the nurses. They asked if I needed anything else and I reassured them that, with my bed back in action, I was good to go. After they realized that I was sane and safe to be left alone, I was back on my own and decided that this whole situation called for some pain medication. I pushed the button and went back to sleep.

The next day Bob was there bright and early and became my constant companion for the remainder of the week. Not being in a local hospital actually became a blessing as infrequent visitors allowed Bob and I to regroup after all the happenings of the past few weeks and allowed me to take frequent, uninterrupted naps, which were very conducive for my healing. We would go on walks in the hallways and then relax and talk. It was during that time that Bob shared with me that, immediately after the surgery while he was driving home, the first thought he had was to call mom and let her know that all was well, only to realize she was no longer there. That created sadness in him, and we both became emotional as we realized that we did not have a moment in the past few weeks to mourn her loss. But I also reassured Bob that God's plan was perfect, because she would have been beyond devastated about this second diagnosis and, furthermore, I was very sure she already knew all was well.

It was also very interesting being a patient as a nurse and, having worked with many incredible nurses during my more than three decades in nursing, I soon saw similarities in the nurses taking care of me and knew without a doubt what the shift was going to be like: most of them good, some not so much. One nurse with a wonderful sense of detail of total nursing care asked if I would like to talk to someone from the clergy department, and I told her I would and to her question who I would like to see I told her to surprise me. Well she did and that afternoon I had a visit from a female Methodist pastor who sat down on the foot of my bed and had just the most beautiful smile. We talked for the longest time, never saying the same thing twice, which my husband has come to realize women can do very easily. She was a true blessed gift that day.

Another nurse insisted that I would agree to have a visiting nurse for a week after I came home, which I told her I did not need, because, after all, I was a nurse. She said she knew that, but now I was a patient first and nurse second and she felt it would be of great benefit to me. How right she turned out to be!

But I must say that my all-time favorite nurse was the one working the 7 P.M. to 7 A.M. shift, which is one of the ones that I have worked and knew about the many challenges it can have. She was a traveling nurse from Florida where her family was currently living. I have worked with many traveling nurses and always found them to be excellent and dedicated nurses. Some of them decided on this to be able to see more of the country, but most did it for economic reasons and to benefit their family back home. They were only able to go back home every few months, which was especially hard for those with husbands and children. But as a parent, you do what needs to be done and they always had my admiration for that sacrifice.

This nurse also helped me during one of my negative experiences. Because I had radiated skin there was a slight chance the tram flap might fail, and to be on the safe side my plastic surgeon had placed me on a five day regimen of intravenous antibiotic treatment. When I did not receive my 4 o'clock dose on the third day, I called my nurse and inquired about that. She told me that the antibiotics were finished, and when I told her about the five day plan she said I was wrong. I started to feel this slight feeling of panic since all had gone so well until now and asked if she could please call my surgeon. She shook her head and told me to relax because she knew what she was doing. Right after this Bob, who had stepped out for a while to make some phone calls, walked back in the room and found me in a puddle of desperation. I told him what had happened and his first inclination was to find my nurse, but I told him that my favorite nurse was coming in early as she wanted to visit with me before her shift started and that she would take care of it. And did she ever! Before I was finished telling her my tale of woe she was back with my antibiotic. I asked how she was able to call the doctor so fast and she said she was planning to call him after she took care of me. She knew of the five day plan and decided that it was more than likely a pharmacy mix-up and she would take care of it all. She was visibly upset that this whole unnecessary situation had even taken place. I later found out that I was not the only one having been on the receiving end of "Nurse Wretched' "nursing skills.

Peace descended once again and I will never forget my traveling nurse's kindness and inspiration for me as a nurse.

Friday of that week was a day with a star. Early morning, my surgeon came in, sat on the foot of the bed and gave me the good news that my nodes were negative. Despite her best plan to have the radioactive dye injected the day before the surgery to facilitate the sentinel node procedure, my radiated tissue held on to it and it never went to the nodes. She went to plan B and removed the sentinel node and three additional nodes at each side. As far as she was concerned, I would not need chemotherapy, maybe Tamoxifen, but suggested I should follow-up with an oncologist in my area just to make sure. We continued to talk for a while, and I could not wait to tell Bob the good news. The rest of the day was spent playing cards, talking and going for the mandatory walks in the hallway. I told Bob that to celebrate I should be allowed to leave the floor and go to the lobby, which was decorated like a garden. To my surprise he said yes and we sneaked off the floor, into the elevator and into the "garden". We sat on one of the benches for a while and just being away from the surgical floor where we had spent most of the week, was the right celebration for this wonderful news.

Later that afternoon two gentlemen came into the room and asked if we wanted communion and we both said yes. I mentioned that I had just found out that my nodes were negative and they said the most beautiful personalized prayer. They admired my by now quite impressive flower collection and I suggested that, since I was going home in two days, for them to take the biggest flower pieces and maybe place them in the chapel. They thanked us and said while they were there they would say an additional prayer of thanksgiving for my good news.

Bob left after dinner and after all the special happenings of the day, I dozed off earlier than expected. I woke up around ten when I felt the gentle touch of a hand on my right arm. It was my plastic surgeon, and I told him that my nodes were negative. He smiled and said, "Ah, cured", and then realizing what time is was I asked him what he was doing in the hospital on a Friday night at ten o'clock, and he said he did not want me to think he forgot about me. Like that would ever happen!

The next day was the day before going home and I started with a slight feeling of anxiety, which I shared with Bob. He listened and then suggested that being in the hospital was in a way a sense of security that if anything happened people were there to take care of it. He promised me that he would do his very best to be my caretaker at home and his analogy and understanding of my feelings helped tremendously in dealing with this unexpected feeling of anxiety. Several special friends we knew from church stopped by in the early evening and were happy to see me doing so well. We talked and laughed and it was perfect timing for their visit as it started the transition from the hospital to "normal" life, whatever that would be.

13

Homeward Bound

Saturday was discharge day and after instructions and saying goodbye to very special care givers, I was on my way home. I remember the drive home very well as it was a beautiful sunny day and everything looked so much better than on the drive almost a week earlier in the other direction.

Being back home felt great and I soon realized I had nothing to worry about. Pumpkin, the cat, welcomed me back with loud meows and did not leave my side. The next day was a beautiful day as well and since Bob had to go to several stores, I decided to go with him and just stay in the car while he went in. I would roll down the window and enjoy the warm sun on my face. It was all good!

It did not take long to settle into a steady routine of following the discharge instructions. Since for the next ten days I was only able to go up and down the stairs once a day, my routine was in the morning to go down two steps to Brian's old room, which I felt did not count. Bob would bring my decaf tea, no caffeine for two weeks after surgery, and an organic muffin a wonderful friend, and survivor as well, had baked and brought to the house. This was the easy part. The other instruction was no shower while the drains were in, and I would wash myself as best as I could and then Bob would step in and wash my back. Then it was slowly down the stairs until bedtime, and the same would be repeated the next day. Once downstairs I would empty my drains and record the output, something as a nurse I was very familiar with.

Monday was back to work for Bob, and after making sure I had everything I needed, he was on his way with the plan to be back for lunch. This was also the first day for my visiting nurse and what a gift she turned out to be. She was kind, compassionate and very thorough when checking to make sure that all was progressing according to plan. I ran into a slight problem in the middle of the week, probably because I had overdone it, and she wasted no times checking with my doctor and putting my mind at ease. We both experienced separation anxiety on her last visit as she mentioned how much of an inspiration I had been to her and I whole heartedly returned that sentiment to her. She gave me a beaded bracelet symbolizing hope and it still has a place of honor on my dressing table.

The week was also filled with flower deliveries and much appreciated homemade meals! Bob would call in the afternoon and ask if he was on for cooking duty that evening and I always had the good news about yet another delivery. All the meals were different and delicious and remembering how helpful it was, especially for Bob, I have made it a habit to do the same for many friends and acquaintances over the years since. Some of my friends had large families and their meals lasted for a while, but one special meal was from a friend who called in the morning to ask what time we usually had supper. I told her the time and she delivered a delicious complete hot meal, including desert, at our usual dinner time. On top of the desert she had taped an index card with a scripture verse from Nehemiah 8:10, which read "The joy of the Lord is your strength". I immediately taped it to the refrigerator and to this day, covered with plastic to secure preservation, it is still a presence in that same area. This verse over the years has become a special mantra to reflect on when times were difficult and I felt my strength being zapped.

I had decided to take a week off from class, but time was up and I emailed my professor to let him know I was good to go, albeit from home, and start class again. I asked if he would he be so kind to tape his Tuesday and Thursday class for me and I told him that my husband would drop off a tape on Tuesday morning and then pick it up in the afternoon and do the same again on Thursday. I thought this was a great idea to keep me involved and an easier reentry to attend class when I had clearance from my doctors to return. I also noticed on the syllabus that a paper was due in a short time and asked about the details on that as well. To the credit of both men, neither one questioned my decision: they just went with it. I guess they had realized by now that would have been an exercise in futility.

It turned out to be the best medicine for me. After my usual routine in the morning, I would listen to the class on the tape and then go behind the computer for several hours. Bob would come home to have lunch with me and after that I would curl up on the couch for a well-deserved nap with my faithful cat purring away next to me.

After a three week period of "home schooling," I returned to class. My plastic surgeon had finally removed my drains, but since I was not allowed to drive as of yet, Bob became my faithful driver and would drop me off before work. Then after class I would walk the small distance to his office and waited until he was able to drive me back home again. Sometimes, time permitting on his part, he would treat me to lunch and it felt so good to be part of the outside world again.

November came and had so many positives to offer. My oncologist did not see any reason for chemo therapy, only a five-year regimen of Tamoxifen, yeah, and to round it off was celebrating Thanksgiving with our kids and extended family in Massachusetts, double yeah!

After Thanksgiving, I received the great news I was allowed to drive again, which made it somewhat easier for Bob even though we truly enjoyed the time of teaming up for the cause.

The time came to get ready for the upcoming holiday season, and something special happened while I was standing in line at the post office to mail a package to my family in Indiana. An elderly man came up to me exclaiming how happy he was to see me and that he had been praying for me since he was at my anointing before my surgery. He kept on shaking my hand and was beaming from ear to ear. I finally recognized him as the man who had given me a medal that had belonged to his late wife and, opening my purse, I showed him that medal pinned to the inside. He smiled even broader and I gave him a big hug. By now we had the attention of pretty much everyone in the post office, but who cared. I was receiving a very special early Christmas gift and the joy of it stayed with me for days.

The healing continued, but I was experiencing more than usual back problems related to a thinner stomach muscle, as half of it was used for my reconstruction and the other half stretched to replace the missing part. Since my back had problems before because of lifting patients during my work as a nurse, this weaker stomach muscle did not help. However, this was still minor as I was so grateful not only that the reconstruction was successful, but most of all that I was alive to enjoy it. I also had learned along the way that everything eventually passes and this would as well.

14

Returning to a "New Normal"

The year 2000 featured a combination of many decisions. Since all had calmed down somewhat, it was time to put mom's house on the market.

We contacted a friend, who was also a Realtor and the house was sold in a reasonable amount of time. She had suggested that the house might sell quicker if it was empty and since I still was not able to do much, after checking what we and the kids would like to have, our friend suggested an in house estate sale to cut down on all the stuff that had been accumulated over the many years. The couple she suggested was very respectful and, aware of the fact this might be difficult for us, did an amazing job. Other items such as furniture were donated to organizations in charge of providing those items to the underserved, which is something mom would have been pleased about. The final part was yet another company who would simply clean out what was left. I could tell that this part of items simply going into plastic bags to be tossed was very difficult for Bob and I suggested he would bring the bags of clothes to be donated to the appropriate donation sites. He gratefully agreed, left with the bags, and returned when the house was empty.

Our son Keith, home for spring break from the boarding school he was teaching at, and one of his friends were "contracted" to paint the inside of the house and did an amazingly professional job.

At the end of the school year, Keith decided to exchange his more rural life in New Hampshire to a job in New York City. He ended up working incredibly long hours, enjoying the challenge of this new job, and also decided to live at home and commute. Bob and I spent most Friday evenings picking up Carrie from the commuter flight from Washington D.C in order for the both of them to be able to spend the weekend together. It was a wonderful summer filled with all positive events. At the end of this summer, Carrie was able to get a job working from home and she and Keith moved to New Rochelle. They both truly enjoyed the opportunity being so close to New York City.

I also was continuing working toward my degree, taking a course in sociology this time, still enjoying the college experience.

Since I had been instructed for as long as possible not to lift anything heavier than a loaf of bread, when laundry was due, Bob would bring the hamper downstairs and after washing the clothes I was actually able to leave it there until he came home and would bring it back upstairs again. Somehow going through eight hours of surgery and subsequent recuperation had made me less anal about many things.

Earlier that year I had also come to the realization that bedside nursing was no longer a possibility and called my supervisor to inform him of that fact. I was offered another position away from the bedside, but, although appreciated, it would not have been the desire of my heart and I decided that after thirty years of service it was time to retire. I went to sign the necessary papers and said hello to my now former coworkers. I knew I had made the right decision, but it was bittersweet cleaning out my locker that I had occupied for so many years. I thought my sadness went unnoticed, but I received a beautiful card a few days later from a very special nurse who had noticed. She wrote that her heart was hurting when she saw how difficult it was for me to leave a place that had been my home away from home for such a long time. She further mentioned that I reminded her of a Black Eyed Susan, which are plants that bloom everywhere under any circumstances and she just knew I would too. I still have that card safely tucked away with other encouraging and heartfelt messages and Black Eyed Susan's have been a presence in our yard ever since. How awesome are these simple acts of kindness!

The decision was also made to go for the final phase of my reconstructive surgery, which was a nipple reconstruction. Since I had experienced some lung problems with the general anesthesia needed for my surgery, related to the damage caused by my radiation treatments, I was able to convince my plastic surgeon once again to use local numbing and intravenous sedation versus general anesthesia for this procedure.

I woke up in the recovery room and Bob was there. He mentioned that my surgeon said all went well and that I probably would not be happy with him as he had to insert drains again, this time sticking out sideways from my hip area! The only positive was that, this time, I would be allowed to take a shower with them in, which made it less of an issue for me.

These drains required a trip to the store to purchase several larger sweaters, and with the culprits tucked in my underwear, covered with a roomy sweater, I was able to continue my daily activities, including going to class, and no one was the wiser. The day finally came that these drains became a thing of the past as well. The next appointment was for a tattoo procedure to fill in the created area with a matching color similar to the other nipple. I was back in my usual costume of no clothes from the waist up, as I watched Bob and my plastic surgeon going over potential color matches. I briefly thought about asking if a tiny butterfly could be added, just for kicks, but did not think I should interrupt their very serious decision making process.

The right color was finally decided upon and Bob and I watched the very unfamiliar process of tattooing. Numbing the area was not necessary as then and even now there is no feeling in that area.

A not so popular decision I decided to make was that it had become high time that Bob and I join Weight Watchers as inactivity and eating out had taken its toll. Bob was not necessarily on board with this one, but decided to be a good sport and join me. I fondly remember one time stepping out of the shower and Bob mentioning how great I looked. He was referring to the weight I had lost, but looking down I saw this large purple incision from hip to hip and a breast that still was trying to figure out what had happened. I mentioned this fact to him and he said that he considered those to be my battle scars and it showed that I had survived the war. I was very impressed about this analogy, and at the same time very touched as this is not a typical thought process for him. We both had grown so much in our relationship, stepping out of our comfort zones with more ease than ever before.

During this time, via a dear friend, I was put in contact with another survivor who, after finishing her treatments, was not able to find any organization in the community to answer the question "what now" and, like Bob did a few years ago, decided to create an organization to give that answer. She called me and during our initial conversation we were on the phone for over an hour, and it felt as if we had known each other for years. I was so impressed with her vision and told her I was in. After several more phone conversations I invited her to speak at my small support group about her vision, and we finally met face to face.

I have always said that she brought the fun into cancer. From fashion shows, with survivors as models, well organized weekend retreats, to support groups with all survivor related topics, she covered it all. I was in the first fashion show and it was such a life giving moment. A local upscale clothing store provided the clothes and there even was someone to do hair and make-up. Here I was, one year after my second diagnosis, surgeries and treatments behind me and my family and a special friend cheering me on in the audience. Bob surprised me with a dozen pink roses and I was hooked on the experience. I immediately volunteered to help with the next fashion shows, as I wanted every survivor to have that same special moment of celebration. After a few years, Bob came on board as the emcee and many funny moments occurred as he was trying to decipher the descriptions of the clothing. Some of the favorites were "who knew there were so many shades of blue and what is boiled wool and why does anyone want to do that?" As you can imagine, a translator ended up assigned to him during the fashion shows to answer these all important questions.

15

Life Goes On

Returning to a "new normal", the next few years were filled with increasing community involvements and working toward my degree. My battle scars were slowly fading, but the meaning of them never forgotten.

I also had volunteered to be available to speak with newly diagnosed women to get them past the very frightening and overwhelming first few days after the diagnosis. Many times this counseling was done by phone which gave the women somehow the added comfort to ask very personal questions. One woman did not want to go to a support group and asked if she could call me once a week and I told her that of course she could. We did that for a year and built a very special friendship. We finally met after that year and even though she has moved away, we are still in contact with each other. Bob volunteered his time to counsel the husbands, which was many times only one phone call. Once the men understood that their feelings of helplessness were a natural reaction to a very difficult situation and then were given a plan of action, they were all set. Sometimes I had to laugh as I would be talking to their wives many more times than that, but somehow that partnership of counseling became helpful and encouraging for many couples going into a battle that we had fought and won for the time being.

The years were a blend of gaining and losing family members. In 2003 Keith and Carrie became engaged and decided to purchase a home in the same town where we were living, which was a real treat to have them so close by. Bob and I, as well as Brian, Kathy and several friends, all pitched in painting and helping with odd jobs that needed to be done to make the house a home. Thanks to all the hard work by many and Carrie's great decorating skills, it succeeded in in no time at all. This gave them the time needed to start making all the arrangements in planning their wedding, which would take place the next year in Scotland.

October of each of those years was the time for the dreaded mammogram, which I always thought, since there was only one breast to be checked, should have been half price, but that logic never followed suit. The surgeon who had performed my mastectomy moved to a hospital outside our area and highly recommended a local surgeon, my third one on the journey. This surgeon was connected with the center that had been so incredible helpful arranging all the details when I was diagnosed for the second time, and I felt it was truly meant to be that I follow that advice. As the previous ones, this surgeon was caring and very understanding about my anxiety regarding the yearly mammogram. One time I mentioned that I was almost sorry not have opted for a bilateral mastectomy since that way I would not have this stress each October. She reassured me that I made the right decision not to do so by calmly explaining the reasons why she felt this way.

In December of 2003 Keith and Carrie decided to move back to England as Keith was offered a wonderful job opportunity. They sold their home and left right after Christmas.

In January 2004 we dealt with the death of Bob's aunt, Helen, and had to make the difficult decision to admit her sister, Roni, to a nursing home as her dementia was progressing. Thankfully, after an initial rocky start with an understaffed facility and Aunt Roni being injured by another patient, we were able to secure a place for her in a wonderful facility where she spent the remaining years of her life, and was given the most amazing care. I would visit her during the week and Bob and I would both see her on the weekend. We had many what we call "Aunt Roni moments" when she would come out with the funniest comments. Initially we would bring her to our home for different occasions, but as her dementia progressed, that was no longer a possibility. Toward the end of her life she would smile when I came to visit, and even though happy to see me, she did not know who I really was. This was very difficult for me as throughout my married life she was my special buddy, and after she retired we would go out many times for lunch and clothes shopping. During my frequent visits to the nursing home, I would look at her and wonder where she went and where people in general go when dementia enters their life. Bob and I were slowly becoming the next generation to carry on the family traditions.

In contrast, June, 2004 will always remain very special for two reasons: my graduation and Keith and Carrie's wedding in Scotland.

My graduation with high honors came first and it was a very emotional and at the same time joyful occasion. My brother, Rokus and sister-in-law, Corrie, Brian and Kathy and a special friend were in attendance as Bob gave me my diploma. This was a total surprise to me and it shows that on the picture the photographer took that evening. It was only fair that Bob would be part of it as he, since my typing skills left a lot to be desired at that time, would faithfully type my papers as he was trying to decipher my hand written notes. Since that became too much of a frustration I decided that it would be easier if I just read them to him and then he could type. I suggested that he could see this as a very special time we were spending together, but I was pretty sure he did not see it as such. He also started calling me the ultimate editor because, until the evening before the paper was due, I would be behind the computer moving things around again. I did get straight A's in all my courses, something amazing to me, but Bob still believed it was way too much effort.

The morning after the graduation Brian and Kathy went back home to Massachusetts to get ready for the wedding in Scotland, and Rokus and Corrie stayed with us for the next two days prior to us all going to Scotland as well. Upon our arrival, we were warmly welcomed by Carrie's parents, Helen and Ian, as well as their extended family and friends.

The wedding was a wonderful celebration of Keith and Carrie's love and so many other things. And even the weather cooperated with bright sunshine with no "Scottish mist" in sight! A total of 54 Americans attended and all the men, except two, wore kilts. Brian did an amazing and very humorous toast to the couple and started it by referring to the time not so long ago his brother had done the same for him and Kathy.

16

My Brother and Me
On the Cancer Journey

I was born two years after World War II. It was a time
for renewal after the nightmare of the German
occupation of the Netherlands had finally ended, and
the country was in the process of re-building, for many
places such as my hometown Rotterdam, from the
ground up. The heart of the city was severely bombed
and many buildings and homes, as well as many lives,
destroyed in the process.

My mother had a miscarriage after my brother was born fourteen years earlier, and because of the constant rumors of war, my parents decided that it might be better not to have another child at this time. However, after the war and encouraged by the positive spirit in the country they made the decision to have another child. My mother required a Dilation and Curettage procedure that was not available after her previous miscarriage, which her doctor believed would increase her changes for a pregnancy. He was right and almost two years after Holland was liberated I was born.

My dad was always a very progressive, "a way ahead of his time" man, and decided he would be present in the delivery room to be a support for my mother. When the doctor told both of them it was a girl, my father got so excited that the doctor had to remind him this he was not at a soccer game but in a delivery room. My father went home via the trolley, still trying to comprehend that the family had the addition of a healthy baby girl. My name was not decided upon as yet, but that occurred on that trolley as well. My father told me the story about a young girl with a blond ponytail, full of life and joy, who hopped and skipped leaving the trolley at her stop, and her friends all yelled "bye Marian, see you tomorrow". He immediately said to himself "that will be her name, because I know that is how she will be". Because it was customary, actually required, to have a grandparent's name as part of a grandchild's name, I was officially named Maria after my grandmother, and Anne after my mother, with a call name of Marian.

Since my mother was forty one, which was an unusual age to have a baby by choice at that time, people would sometimes inquire if I was an "accident". I did not know what that meant, but I did not like it when that was mentioned, and for years if someone would ask me my name I would say "My name is Marian, and I am not an accident"!

My brother was almost 17 when I was born, and I was sure a baby sister was not at the top of a teenager's wish list, especially a precocious one as I was called at times, which could be translated as "an in your face, pain in the neck." I followed my brother all through the house and when I was around 6 years old I figured out that when he was not home he was most likely at his girlfriend's Corry's house. I would load up my doll carriage with my favorite dolls, marched right over to her house and announced my presence. Although Corry and her family always welcomed me with open arms, I am sure my brother must have thought at times that "there is just no getting away from this girl"

The first change in our relationship came when I was 9. My brother married Corry and they moved to America. At that time phone calls were at a minimum and we were only able to connect during infrequent visits that for me went by way too fast. Then life for both of us began to change as well as I became busy with nursing school and Rokus with building his career.

I spent some time with Rokus, Corry and their son Michael when I was 16 and we connected again when I was 21 and decided to immigrate to America. Rokus, still seeing me as his little sister, was understandably worried about me and tried to discourage my plans to immigrate. However, he slowly started to realize that I had grown beyond being his "little follower" and became very proud of my accomplishments.

Getting married and becoming a parent as well, the years between us seem to matter less and less. However, during the seven years when both of us started taking turns walking our cancer journeys, the years simply disappeared. We shared our fears and anxieties about upcoming tests, supported and encouraged each other when the results were not what we hoped for and rejoiced when they were.

January, 2005, brought cancer into my life again on another level. I received a call from Corrie that my brother was having pains in his stomach not relieved by antacids, and what did I think it could be? I was not sure and gave some suggestions about possible causes never in a million years anticipating what it turned out to be. After several tests my brother was diagnosed with esophageal cancer. He called me with the news and since both of us had successfully beaten several cancers he was positive this would happen again.

Our cancer journey started when I was diagnosed with breast cancer, then he followed me with prostate cancer, and I followed that with my second bout of breast cancer. I remember telling him that this was pure sibling rivalry, but I was done, and he was the winner. We both laughed expecting a full discovery. Sadly, this time around, despite incredible efforts, it was not the case.

Rokus went through chemo therapy treatments, which initially had great results and the tumor all but disappeared. The next step was surgery to remove the esophagus and create a new one by pulling up the stomach and attaching it to the throat area. Despite his age, he was in great physical condition and decided to proceed with the recommended surgery. Since I had known several people that had gone through this same surgery and were all doing well, I fully supported his decision to do so.

After his surgery in April it became a very tough road for him. Eating solid food was very difficult and his throat had to be stretched frequently, which was apparently not an unusual occurrence after this type of surgery. I was in constant contact with both him and Corry and decided to visit for a while to encourage him. Both of us were still hopeful and had many special conversations during that visit. Although in obvious discomfort, he never, ever complained and made the most of each day.

17

It Just Never Seems Enough

As had happened before, this apparently was not enough to be happening at this time. In July of that same year an ultrasound of my uterus and ovaries looked suspicious and biopsies of these areas were scheduled.

Once again, Bob was left in the waiting room, and when I was walking through the hallway with the nurse I decided to ask if it would be possible to have my husband in the room during the procedure. Fully expecting a resounding "No, not possible" she surprised me by saying that my doctor welcomed that type of support and if I thought my husband could handle it, he was more that welcome to join the party. I quickly went back to the waiting room and said, "Guess what, the nurse said that you can come with me", like I was inviting him to a special event instead of what was about to happen. I think Bob did view it that way as he jumped up, relieved not to have to sit there and worry about me. What could have been another stressful time changed into an almost "nonevent" because of the kindness of my doctor and her staff.

Since this was a relative new procedure, another doctor joined the team as an observant, and he and my husband were treated to step by step details of this procedure. Bob decided at one point to mention that, as a freshman in college, he declared a major in pre-med, but did not pursue it after that year. A lively discussion followed and I asked at one point if they realized I was still there, in a very compromising position no less. They all assured me they were aware, Bob now part of the team.

After the procedure, I had to lay flat for quite a while and I turned to Bob and told him that no matter what the outcome was, I was going to have surgery and take care of this problem once and for all. He said that maybe we should talk about this further, but he already knew in his heart that as far as I was concerned, this was not up for discussion. My doctor came back in the room and I told her the same. She explained the option to be "watched closely" with frequent ultra sounds, but I told her, with everything else going on, I would prefer not to go that route. She gently touched my arm and said, "I don't blame you, when you would like the surgery". Since she was eight months pregnant at that time, I said, "How about yesterday, and definitely before you have that baby". She laughed and said she would see what she could do.

Even though the biopsies came back negative for cancer, one of my tumor markers came back high normal and I knew I had made the right decision to have a total hysterectomy and bilateral oophorectomy. I reassured Bob by saying that I had this gut feeling that if I did not do this now, I was sure it would come back to haunt me as I had this strong feeling it had all the makings of yet another cancer. He respected my gut feeling and was more at ease about yet another surgery.

I had decided not to mention any of this to my brother and sister-in-law until all the details were in and a plan of action was put into place, and I decided to do the same with Keith and Carrie in England. I had learned early on with parents in Holland that distance magnified problems and they were much easier to deal with when a plan was in place and questions could be answered. I called my brother, told him what the problem was, and how it was going to be taken care of. He totally agreed with my decision to go for the surgery and thereby preventing yet another cancer the opportunity to start.

Next, I called my children and informed them about the situation. They were concerned, as Bob was, about another surgery, but I was able to reassure them as well that this had to be done to allow me to go on living my life without the stress of constant tests. They understood, and as before, I asked Brian to be there for his dad, and this time his wife Kathy offered to come as well. Both worked mostly from home and since they would be able to rearrange their work schedule, the plan was to stay for a few days this time.

The usual pre-operative tests were scheduled. I gave my cell phone number to the staff with the hope of getting a call for a surgery date very soon. Thankfully, that happened within a week and I was scheduled for surgery on Tuesday, July 26.

We went for a final visit with my MD to go over the details of the surgery and an opportunity to ask any additional questions we might have. I just had one, and it was not surgery related. The daughter of a close friend was getting married on August 13 in Washington D.C., and since the surgery was way more than a week before that, I would like to go to that wedding as I saw no reason that we should not go. She said she would seriously consider it and gave me a tentative yes. That was a definite yes for me and I finally returned the response card to the bride to be with a smiley face on it.

The day before the surgery included a liquid diet, followed by a colon prep similar to the one before going for a colonoscopy. My doctor had ordered this by a slim chance that one or both of my ovaries were imbedded into the colon necessitating a colon resection. Who knew that this could even happen? Having gone through this prep before I knew it was not going to be fun and decided that a pedicure was in order prior to starting it.

I choose my favorite nail polish color called "Dutch Tulips" and, with my newly painted toes in a beautiful happy red, it was much easier to follow doctor's orders.

My surgery the next day was not scheduled until late morning, and Brian and Kathy arrived around nine o'clock that morning. When they came I was dressed in a long, comfortable summer dress and with my newly pedicured toes I must say I looked pretty good. Kathy looked at me and said, "I don't believe this; you look like you are going to the beach instead of surgery". I told her that achieving success of just about everything was all in the attitude and we laughed.

This time around I was in a local hospital in the town I lived in and we were there within ten minutes. The admitting process started and, once again, I was the same blue attire as several years ago. The anesthesiologist came in and asked the familiar questions and I mentioned that my only problem with anesthesia had been nausea, which would linger for a while. He said that could be taken care of and ordered some medications by mouth to be given prior the surgery. His last question was if I was Swedish and I told him I was Dutch. He said he could never tell as we all sounded alike, and I told him that we Europeans did that on purpose to confuse the Americans. He laughed and said, "Good one, see you later". So far I was two for two with anesthesiologists with a sense of humor. After getting hugs from Bob, Brian and Kathy I was wheeled into the operating room.

This time there was an extra aspect to deal with because of my previous tram flap surgery. A plastic surgeon was on standby to make sure that no blood vessels providing the needed blood flow to my reconstructed breast would be nicked during this surgery. It was also explained to me that during surgery frozen sections of the ovaries would go to the lab to be checked for cancer cells as in that case several lymph nodes in the area would have to be removed. I was so glad to be sleeping when this was all going on!

Thanks to the pre-operative medication I woke up with just a slight nausea this time, which subsided much faster that the last time around. Since this was a much shorter surgery than the previous one, the waiting time was much easier on my family as well.

After a short time in the recovery room, I was able to see my family who had already been given the good news that my ovaries were negative for cancer cells and no lymph node removal had been necessary. My surgery had gone even better than expected and I should have an uncomplicated recovery. Now that was news worth waking up for!

I was wheeled to my room and my family stayed by my side until I was barely able to keep my eyes open. I suggested for them to go and have dinner and I was asleep before they even left the room. I had a great sleep and Bob returned to stay with me for most of the evening.

As in my previous hospital stay, I encountered "the best and not so" nurses. Again, I was blessed on the first night with a traveling nurse taking care of me. She was kind and I knew I was in good hands and had nothing to worry about. I remember my back being sore and felt a walk might help. When my nurse came in to check my vital signs a second time, I asked her if she had time to take me for a walk. She was amazed that I wanted that so soon after my surgery, but said if I felt I was up to it, she was too. So there we were at four o'clock in the morning, walking the halls of the hospital, pushing an IV pole with my catheter attached to it in one hand, and my other arm linked to the arm of this wonderful nurse. It did wonders for my back and I was able to fall back into a restful sleep.

Bob came in early the next morning and I told him all was going great and that he should go to work. He was hesitant but I assured him that this time it was a very different scenario than last time. My intravenous and catheter were going to be removed that morning, which made me a pretty independent patient. He finally agreed with the promise of coming back at lunch time.

Kathy decided to come in during the afternoon and said she came without the men because she wanted to make sure for herself that everything was as good as I said it was. I reassured her that it was and we spent a nice time talking. All three of them came back to visit early evening and, as the previous night; I suggested they go out for dinner. Since Bob was planning to come back after that I asked him to bring me back an ice cream Sunday with all the bells and whistles.

Regretfully, my second evening and night was not like the first one. My angel from the night before came to my room and told me that her request to have me as a patient again was denied by the nurse in charge, but that she would check in as often as she could. As she was new to this department, I did not want her to get in trouble and told her I would be fine and for her to be careful. Well, apparently it is a requirement for every hospital to have a "Nurse Wretched" and she was mine again, and again an issue with antibiotics. What are the chances! She came into my room and told me that I would not have my favorite nurse, but her instead. Thankfully, I did not see much of her during the evening shift and, since I was much more independent that time, it was not a problem. I waited until Bob came back from dinner and then called her to let her know that I did not receive my six P.M. intravenous antibiotic. She insisted it was not due until ten and I did not have the energy to argue with her. She came back at ten while Bob was still there and I had to call her again when it was finished and the blood was backing up in the catheter. I knew that unless it was flushed soon the line would clog and unable to be used for the remainder of the ordered antibiotics.

Bob left and I dozed off only to be woken up by the night nurse who was going to give me my twelve midnight antibiotic. I told her that my last dose was given at ten and she said that I was wrong because it was charted for 6 P.M. by my evening nurse. I told her that my husband was here at ten and I would be very happy to call him to verify that my facts were correct. She became annoyed with at me, who had not caused this problem, and I suggested she would give this dose around two A.M. and then my last dose could then be given later in the morning. She knew it was a definite it was not happening now and came back around two in the

116

morning. Since the previous small bag of antibiotics had almost run dry, there was a large amount of air in the tubing. I asked her to please flush that out, but she said a little air was not a problem. However, it was a problem for me and a plan of action was in order. I waited until she left the room and closed off the flow before the air had a chance to enter my vein. This was the easy part, as now I had to figure out how to disconnect the tubing from the needle, which was in my left hand, only having my right hand to do so, and no extra hand available to make sure I did not pull the whole needle out. I finally decided that the best way was to hold the needle in place with my right hand and disconnected the tubing with my teeth, flush the air out and then reconnect it. The plan was successfully executed! It was also at this time I decided to tell my doctor it was time to go home a day early as staying in this hospital would not be good for my physical or emotional health.

I decided not to go into details with my doctor, but was definite about leaving that day. Thankfully, the day nurse was wonderful and made the previous experiences a thing of the past.

I went home on a beautiful sunny day and treasured sitting out on the back deck. Brian and Kathy were still there, hard at work, and we enjoyed a delicious home cooked dinner before they returned back to their home that evening.

Two days later, three dear friends came to visit and brought coffee, muffins and gifts. They wanted to see for themselves that I was well and we were all sitting outside having a great time. What a difference scenario from last time!

Since I was still bargaining for the wedding in Washington D.C., I suggested to Bob that we should go to a neighborhood party that evening for a while so that he could see for himself that all was well. I promised that I would take a nap that afternoon, but I just got a look of slight desperation. We went to the party and I told Bob upon our return that the caring attitude of neighbors was just what the doctor ordered, and again that look.

My follow up appointment was the next Monday and again nothing but good news. All the lab results had come back negative for cancer cells. I reminded my doctor about her permission to go to the wedding and she hesitated somewhat. Finally she said, "OK, but absolutely no lifting of any kind and no dancing on tables". I told her that last one might be difficult to do as that was my specialty. She gave me a "Bob" look and I quickly told her I was just kidding.

The wedding was wonderful as many of our friends were there as well. Since a heat wave was taking place that weekend, we only ventured out once for me to get a manicure, and spend the rest of the time either attending several scheduled wedding related functions, or playing cards in our room. It was a very special weekend celebrating a very special couple.

Upon our return, I continued the recuperation process and now referring to my stomach as a "holy belly" as a vertical incision line had been added to the previous horizontal one. It looked like everything had finally calmed down for me and my family.

However, much more was to come.

18

Sometimes Love and Encouragement are not Enough

I had been in contact with my brother and it seemed that everything was improving for him as well. He even had gone back to a part-time job he really enjoyed. During one of our phone calls, he mentioned that a daughter of Dutch friends was getting married in Pennsylvania and he and Corry were debating about going. I suggested that they should go and then come and visit us for a while. He decided that was a good idea and plans for a visit, we were all looking forward to, were made. I was so happy that we would be able to spend time together and put the cancer journeys behind us. Again, best laid plans.....

I received a call from Corry the night before the wedding with the news that Rokus was in a hospital in Pennsylvania with a possible obstruction. She was crying and I was doing my best to comfort her. I also started to get this nagging feeling that something bigger was brewing and tried to put that out of my mind. Rokus had told her to go to the wedding and she did not know what to do. I told her that would be the best thing to do as there was nothing she could do for my brother and he needed his rest. I suggested that one of her Dutch friends should pick her up and leave their cell phone number for the hospital staff in case they needed to get in touch with her. Reassured that I agreed with Rokus, she went, and being surrounded by familiar faces, was able to take her mind of this whole situation for a while.

I spoke with Rokus the next day and no plan of discharge was planned as of yet. I told him not to worry, because as soon as he had a discharge date, Bob was planning to fly out to Pennsylvania and drive both of them back to our home in my brother's car. This flying idea was wrought with some problems, such as, "you cannot get there from here" situations, but we decided to figure that out when the time came. I mentioned all this to a good friend who called to see how I was doing. She could not believe the continuing sage in my life and told me to tell Bob not to worry about flying because her husband, one of Bob's best friends, would be happy to drive Bob there on the day my brother would be discharged. I called my brother to let him know and he was very overwhelmed and touched about the willingness of our friends to come to their aid.

As we were waiting for news about my brother's discharge we almost forgot it was our anniversary that week and Bob decided to make a reservation at our favorite restaurant. The night before our anniversary from out of nowhere I get this shooting pain in my left jaw, which after persisting required a visit to the dentist the next day. And what do you know, I needed a root canal, and why not. The area was too sensitive to be completed during that visit, but the dentist was able to remove the problem area and then packed it. The nurse told me that my jaw would be numb for quite a while and I assured her that "numb was good". I went home and called Bob at work to let him know that I was pain free and good to go for our anniversary dinner. We also heard from my brother that he would be discharged the next day and that was not an issue with a perfect plan in place.

The next day Bob and his friend left early to pick up my brother and sister-in-law and Bob returned later that afternoon with both of them. I did not know what I expected, but it was obvious my brother had spared me some details about his health status. He was skin and bones as he came through our front door and, thankfully, wrapped his arms around me, which gave me time to deal with what I just saw and put my reassuring "nurse face" on.

They initially were planning to stay for a week, but we told them to stay as long as they wanted which was gratefully accepted. The following weeks were spent finishing the root canal procedure, and just relaxing and enjoying each other's company. I also came to realize that my brother was not progressing like the other people I knew with this same surgery, but decided to only focus on the fact that we were together at this time and place.

One morning Rokus and I were talking about the fact that we truly were not good sick people. We do not like it when our life gets interrupted because of illness and how truly blessed we were that we had such loving, patient partners. We also laughed and wondered if we were pushing the envelope on that last one.

And that brings me to Corry, the love of my brother's life. They had met when she was fourteen and he was sixteen and were together ever since that time. My mom was pregnant with me while they were dating and as a small child I truly adored Corry. I thought she was the kindest and most beautiful person in the world. As an adult, I came to realize she was the kindest and she was beautiful because it came from the inside.

I cannot begin to tell you what an inspiration Corry was during those few weeks. Her unconditional love, encouragement and patience were truly amazing and made my husband and me reflect on how we would deal if experiencing that same situation when there did not seem to be a positive end in sight.

After several weeks, the time had come that Rokus and Corry decided to venture going back home. We all tried to discourage my brother taking this long trip home by car and suggested different options, but being stubborn and Dutch that was a no go. I remember the morning they left very clearly: Rokus looking so frail when getting into the car and Corry with tears in her eyes. As soon as they were out of sight I broke down, and asked God to please protect them and give them a safe drive home. Thankfully, by the grace of God and my brother using all the strength he had left, they did.

My brother, at my advice, had made an appointment with his doctors to check why he was just not improving as he should. The results of this visit certainly did not turn out what either one of us hoped for. Rokus called me and said that he had good news and bad news. The good news being that the doctors knew what the problem was, and the bad news that his cancer had spread to his liver. It was apparently something that had been missed during previous scans. Needless to say, I was quite ticked off this serious problem was not discovered earlier, but my brother calmed me down. As far as he was concerned, he was glad he did not know earlier, because Corry would have missed a wonderful time with her Dutch friends at the wedding and he would have missed the very special time we were able to spend together at my home. He added that more than likely the outcome would have been the same as he was then and now to weak for future chemo. I guess there was just no arguing with that outlook and I asked him if he was given a time frame, not really wanting to know the answer. The answer came in the form of two weeks!

I suggested that I would come to Indiana and be with him and Corry, but he said we should focus on the time we had spent living and he did not want me to be there during the time of his dying.

All the encouragement, positive attitude and love did not work this time. This cancer somehow seemed to be stronger that the both of us and it started taking away my confidence.

I had to start focussing on what it could not take away, and came upon the following reflection that became a comfort as it truly described how Rokus was dealing with all the difficulties in his life. It read:

> Cancer is so limiting
>
> It cannot cripple love
> It cannot shatter hope
> It cannot corrode faith
> It cannot destroy peace
> It cannot kill friendship
> It cannot suppress memories
> It cannot silence courage
>
> *And then my favorite:*
>
> It cannot invade the soul
> It cannot conquer the spirit
> It cannot steal eternal life

Since no further treatments were indicated at this time, my brother decided that he wanted to go home and hospice was initiated. Regretfully, his hospice care was, in my opinion, very underwhelming compared to the ones I have seen in my area. Many times I had to give my poor sister-in-law instructions over the phone on how to connect and disconnect intravenous tubing and other details left up to her with minimal explanations and instructions. Given the fact Corry had no medical background of any kind she did amazingly well learning and dealing with this new assignment in her life. My brother was a necessary active participant as well during the times he was not sure if the hospice staff knew what they were doing. He told me once that "some are fine, but with others it is important that I stay awake to make sure they don't mess things up". Somehow this whole situation was incomprehensible to me and did not allow much time for him and Corry to simply being together without these responsibilities. But as long as they had me to check with, they were both dealing amazingly well with this incredible difficult situation and, after I contacted hospice and speaking with some of the staff without any improvement, it was time for me to let it go and focus on what was needed at the moment. This was only on the back burner for the moment as I addressed this debacle of hospice care with the people in charge after my brother passed away, if only to avoid it for someone else without family backup. Corry received an apology after her husband's death, which we both decided was too little too late, but it also allowed us to move on.

The next two weeks were spent with daily phone calls to my brother. In the morning, I would call to ask how his night was and then in the evening about his day and all it had brought. One time, he shared that he might have overwhelmed Corry by explaining too much and too fast how to take care of things after he was gone and she had gotten upset with him. He said he needed to slow down and I assured him not to worry as Bob and I would always be there for his family. He simply answered "if I was only so sure of everything else in my life".

Since the cancer was progressing and he knew his time was limited, our conversations took on a very different direction than before. As the older brother he took the time to give me advice about what mattered and what did not, and, despite the circumstances, we had wonderful conversations. The content of our conversations reminded me of something I had read many years ago in Henri Nouwen's book about death and dying. It mentioned that when people know they are dying, the conversations become very real and honest because all one has is today, as the past no longer matters and the future is no longer there. I remember how reading it touched me, never even imagining I would be experiencing it at a future time.

My brother and I had very different personalities, him the introvert, and me not so much. The advice he gave me during that difficult time, which has helped me the most, was the following. My brother told me, "I know that you need to be out there, be involved and make a difference, but promise me one thing, when you are involved with something that is giving you stress instead of joy, please promise me to get out". This advice has been very instrumental in my decision making process in the past 9 years, and has helped shortening the time agonizing about it as I am still a work in progress.

Many other calls were with Corry and my nephew, Michael, as they were trying to deal with the inevitable outcome and it was a comfort for them to be able to share their sadness with me.

Very close to the time given by his doctor, I received the call from Corry that Rokus had passed away, and Bob and I made the travel plans to be with his family at the funeral. As with all the previous times of loss, Bob, at one time one of his newspaper's obituary writers at the start of his career, wrote the obituary, and I gave a eulogy.

My brother might have lost his battle with cancer but, he fought the good fight, finished the race and, most importantly, he kept the faith. And it is because of this faith that I still know where he is and in God's perfect time I will see him again. He is just getting a little break from me.

One of my brother's favorite poems was "The Road Less Traveled" by Robert Frost and, by reflecting on this poem, I realized that my brother and I took the road less traveled and that had made all the difference.

19

My "Sister" Corry

I had suggested to Bob that we should add on a fewo extra days after my brother's funeral as Corry might need our help sorting through some of the details that needed to be taken care off. This turned out to be a good idea and Bob patiently explained what needed to be done, writing everything out for her on a legal pad, making sure Corry understood.

Given the fact that they were married almost fifty years when my brother died and he had always taken care of all the financials, it became quite an adjustment for Corry to take over this responsibility. But as usual, she rose up to the task at hand, and knowing she could call us anytime was of great help for her.

I decided to go back for a visit a month later, which Corry was very happy about, to help out with many more details that needed to be taken care of and being there in person would be helpful. She was understandably still very sad about her loss, but making small strides to adjust to her "new normal".

I tried to spend time with her whenever I could and during my last visit in January of 2007, I was encouraged to see that she was doing much better. Thanks to a wonderful neighbor, she was stepping out more, something definitely not in her previous comfort zone. She went on some bus trips and other events, always calling me first if I thought that would be a good idea. I always told her to go for it and she did!

We spent our time during my visit in January reminiscing, laughing, and going out for dinner. We even started a slight remodeling project by picking out new furniture for the family room. Because of my fascination with HGTV, I had learned a lot about decorating and we drew up a plan and brought it to the store. I am not sure if the person in the furniture store trying to assist us was equipped to handle two Dutch women, but he certainly got points for trying. We tried out just about every piece of furniture in the store, and by the end could not stop laughing. It was an awesome visit and I promised to come back in the spring to see the finished project for myself. Again, best laid plans...

About a week later, I received a call from my nephew Michael around 10 P.M. He lived about forty five minutes away from his mother and always called her in the evening to make sure all was well. He finally got worried after leaving several messages without a return call and decided to call a neighbor. The neighbor checked through the window and saw Corry lying unresponsive on the kitchen floor. She immediately called the police, ambulance and Michael, who called me and then jumped in his car to drive to his mother's home.

I had told Michael to call me as soon as he had some news and stayed up waiting for his call. At this time neither one of us knew if it was a break-in or something else. Bob had woken up hearing the phone and I updated him on what I knew at this time. We both were just numb and trying not to think the worst.

It turned out to be not a break-in but something else: Michael called us with the news that Corry had experienced a massive stroke, which took her speech and the use of the whole left side of her body. She also sustained a fractured hip in the process of falling.

The next weeks were spent on many phone calls between Michael and us as his mom was going through many tests and procedures to evaluate the extent of the damage. The news was not good as the likelihood of her regaining speech or movement on her left side was deemed highly unlikely. In order to give Corry all the benefits of a more independent life, physical therapy was initiated with less than minimal results. The greatest hinder and big frustration for her was her inability to speak and verbalize what she wanted to say.

With no other options left, the difficult decision had to be made to find an appropriate nursing home for Corry. This was a very unfamiliar road for my nephew and frequent long distance calls were made to help him weave through the maze of finding the one that would best serve his mom. Besides advice what to look for, I also suggested that it should be close to his home as I had learned from experience that problems requiring notifying family members usually happen during the night.

To say that Michael stepped up to the plate was an understatement. He became the voice for his mother during the ups and downs of nursing home life for her. It was not an easy road, but I was very proud how he handled everything, as in essence, he had now lost both parents.

With no improvement in sight for his mom, I had to start talking about the fact that he probably should look into selling his parents' house, and when the time was right for him, he agreed. The house sold quickly, which was unusual as the housing market was not the best at that time, but made the decision so much easier for Michael. I told him to let me know when the closing was and I would come to help him with the necessary sorting and cleaning out of all the stuff accumulated over the years. Michael at first said that he probably could handle it, but I assured him that I had cleaned out many houses and it was a very daunting job for one person. He gratefully accepted my offer and flight reservations were made.

The week I spent there was filled from early morning until late evening. Michael would meet me at the hotel and then we would have a large breakfast to sustain us for most of the day. After that we went full force ahead to accomplish our task of sorting and cleaning the house and at the end of each day we always spent several hours with Corry in the nursing home. She initially did not recognize me and when she finally did, and not able to verbalize, she cried a lot. It was very overwhelming for me to see her like that, but that did not deter me from the daily visits. I finally was able to see a smile on her face after I did her nails and organized some of her clothes and drawers. One day during that week, she had a questioning look on her face and tried to ask something. I surmised that she probably was wondering what was going on. I held her hand and gently told her that when she was a little better, she could not go back to her home because of the stairs and therefore the house had to be sold. I furthermore mentioned that I was here to help Michael clean out the house and that he was taking most of her furniture to his house for safe keeping should she be in need of it at a later date. She nodded that she understood, smiled, and padded my hand. We probably both knew that none of this would happen, but wanting to believe it somehow gave comfort to both of us.

After a record cleaning of the house on Thursday I asked Michael if he felt that he could handle the remaining things to be done, and when he responded affirmative I told him to meet me for lunch at the hotel this time. We then planned to spend the remainder of the afternoon with Corry before my flight back home.

I remember the next morning sitting in my bed trying to process this very sad and emotional week, and I was truly starting to wonder where God was in all this. As a matter of fact that was just what I asked Him when the phone rang. It was a three way call between my husband and Keith in England, and my son said, "Congratulations, you are now grandparents". I said, "What did we have" as Keith and Carrie decided not to know the sex of the baby beforehand, and he said, "A girl". Bob and I were beyond surprised and delighted as our family does only boys.

After we hung up, I had my answer where God was and that His plans are not our plans no matter how hard they are to comprehend at times. I was reminded of Ecclesiastes 3:1 "For everything there is a season, and a time for every purpose under heaven"

Corry passed away on Memorial Day and we returned to Indiana for the funeral. Once again, Bob wrote the obituary and I did the eulogy for Corry, my "sister", as in my mind she was always was much more than a sister-in-law.

20

A Spirit of Gratitude

Here we are, seventeen years after the initial start of my journey. Bob has since retired and we both enjoy our many community involvements, spending time together, as well with our children and, above all, our grandchildren.

The encouraging highway sign Bob and I saw on our way to the hospital so many years ago has come to fruition. We are now the proud Oma and Papa of a beautiful granddaughter, Chloe Catherine, and a handsome -- his words – grandson, Bradley Keith. Just thinking about the two on them fills our hearts with love and joy.

Thankfully, the grandchildren's family now lives a few towns over and airplanes are no longer needed to visit them and our favorite grand dog, Fred. It is nice to be able to visit or help out by taking the little ones and dog overnight to give their parents a well-deserved break.

Looking back over these last seventeen years, I have come to the realization that no one goes it alone, and I have this deep spirit of gratitude for what I call my three F's: My faith, my family and my friends:

Gratitude for my God: who throughout my life has either shielded me from suffering, or has given me unfailing strength to deal with whatever was placed in my path.

Gratitude for my family: first and foremost my parents. By their example, my parents taught me to get involved whenever and wherever there was a need, and always do it from the heart. They also encouraged me to always do the right thing, no matter what the cost might be. My mom also truly believed that when you left this world it had to be a little better because you were in it, otherwise all you had done was take up space. Neither one of my parents ever took up space except for a big one in my heart.

Gratitude for my husband: who always gives me his quiet strength, his unconditional love and unwavering support for everything I get involved in. The latter one is not as easy as it sounds because more often than not it means that, at some level, I get him involved as well.

Gratitude for my two sons: not only for the caring men they have grown up to be, always being there when it really matters, but also for choosing such incredible life partners. These wonderful young women have given the much appreciated female touch to my all male household and I could not love them more if they were my own.

Then our family was blessed with the very special additions of a now seven year old granddaughter and four year old grandson. They are kind, funny and the joy of my life, and just thinking about them brings a smile to my heart.

I am also so very grateful for my friends, who I call friends for all seasons as they were not just around when the days were warm and sunny, but stayed around when the days of life became dark and cold.

Someone once told me that after having experienced cancer, for while it is right in front of you, then it sits on your shoulder as a reminder, and finally it takes more of a backstage role in your life, only to make a re-appearance when an unusual pain or yearly test is upon you. You somehow are never the same again, but I do not think that is a necessarily bad thing.

Two thought processes have been very helpful for me. The first one is that when I add all my blessings, the pile is so high that the cancer is no longer visible. Cancer has also made me realize how strong my faith is, how enriched my marriage has become, and how blessed I am with my children, grandchildren, extended family and special friends. Any difficult journey is always so much easier when you are not traveling it alone.

Secondly, each morning when I get up with both feet above ground I consider it a good day. And to think that something as ugly as cancer could accomplish all that!

I also have come to realize that everyone's journey is different and many people do get stuck along the way.

However, it has been my experience that if I meet that person where they are on their journey with acceptance, understanding and compassion, many times I have been able to fill their half empty glass just enough to encourage them to continue the journey.

Yes, by the grace of God, my glass is still always half full and my "new normal" has been tremendously blessed.

Made in the USA
Middletown, DE
08 June 2023